THE MISSING WILL

THE MISSING WILL

——

Michael Wharton

CHATTO & WINDUS

THE HOGARTH PRESS

LONDON

First published in 1984 by
Chatto & Windus   The Hogarth Press
40 William IV Street
London WC2N 4DF

British Library Cataloguing in Publication Data
Wharton, Michael, *1913–*
The missing will.
1. Wharton, Michael, *1913–*   2. Journalists
——Great Britain——Biography
I. Title
070'.92'4   PN5123.W4

ISBN 0-7011-2666-3

Parts of this book were first published
in the *Daily Telegraph* and the *Sunday Telegraph*,
with whose kind permission they are reproduced.

Photoset by Rowland Phototypesetting Ltd
Bury St Edmunds, Suffolk
Printed in Great Britain by
Redwood Burn Ltd
Trowbridge, Wiltshire

To Nicholas

RIDENDUM . . . IUBES RENOVARE DOLOREM

Contents

I
The Deformative Years

My earliest memories of Wharton are of a time when I did not know that any other place existed: the great house, where, in its different styles, the whole history of English domestic architecture could be traced; the terraced gardens; the smooth green lawns; the long avenues of ancient elm, beech and oak leading the eye to the bridge and the double lake; the deer-park; the 'wilderness', meticulously planned by 'Mad Wharton' in the eighteenth century to suggest, at least to his own infatuated eye, all that he liked best among the landscapes of England, ranging in their different styles from the fens of Lincolnshire to the crags of Cumberland; and beyond these vast domains, in the hazy distance, whatever a child's mind might fancy of possible outer worlds.

More intimately known – at least to these flashes of uncertain memory – are the great kitchen gardens with their walls of old red brick (said by an amateur 'antiquarian' uncle to date back to the time of the large Roman villa which sixteen hundred years before had occupied one small corner of the present house). These gardens, tended by an army of gardeners, produced the finest peaches, nectarines and pears in England, to say nothing of the once celebrated Wharton Apple, with its subtle flavour, sharp and sweet, which seemed to include all possible fructose tastes in one.

There was the Long Gallery in which, by some oversight of nursemaid or governess, I once strayed, to be found (so I was told later) dazzled and overwhelmed by the innumerable pictures in which could be traced the whole history of European art since Byzantine times; then taken back, half fainting with precocious ecstasy, to the nursery wing.

There was the nursery wing itself, larger than many a sizeable gentleman's house, where I played with my bricks and little engines or listened to stories of ogres, dragons and peasants (or 'people', as the only nanny I remember at all vividly, Nanny Forbes from Elgin, used to call them, striving, as was her duty, to inculcate in me at an early age a consciousness of their complete difference from such beings as myself).

I remember too, the small four-poster bed in which I slept, five hundred years old, the gift of King Edward IV to my Yorkist ancestor, with its elaborately carved oaken frame, its sumptuous coat-of-arms with sixty-four quarterings at the head, its canopy and curtains of convoluted velvet, disposing me to a habit of vivid dreaming which I have never lost. Even at the age of four, I am told, I used to long for bedtime and the dreams it would bring, dreams in which supernatural splendours, exceeding only by a little the magnificence of my real surroundings, mingled with intimations of other worlds in which Nanny Grant's 'people' would sometimes disconcertingly appear, old, ugly, bent, misshapen, stretching out arthritic hands as though begging for release from mean streets where rain of inferior quality fell forever.

Have I no early memories of – let us call them the 'personages', since nothing less will do – of my own family? They are vague compared with my memories of the great park and all that it contained. I remember my father, a huge, distant, rumbling figure; my mother, scented, elegant, her voice a melodious chime which seemed to mingle with the sound of the French clocks which struck the quarters in the long, sleepy, summer afternoons (by a household rule they never struck in winter). I glimpsed her once drawing on long gloves for some dinner party, perhaps, when fifty guests would be at table in the stupendous dining-room with its phantasmagoria of crystal and silver. I remember that glimpse because to my surprise a single tear fell from her left eye.

How was I to know that the piece of paper she held in her hand

– distastefully crumpled, dirty and out of place even to my child's eye – was a 'telegram' just arrived from the War Office to announce the death of my elder brother the Viscount in action on the Western Front? I imagine, wrongly perhaps, that the dinner party went on. Grief would come later, and would be apparent only to a few.

It may seem odd to say this. But far more vivid in my memory than father, mother, brother, sister or even Nanny Findlay is an experience I had when I was five, perhaps, one autumn afternoon. There was a part of the gardens where I had been told never to go. It was the Maze, said to be the largest and most complicated in England. According to my 'antiquarian' uncle it had originally been laid out by druids to delude and confuse the Roman legions advancing through Britain to enforce, among other things, the abolition of the druidic order.

Into this sinister and complex diagram of tall beech hedges, trimmed by special gardeners who could be relied on not to 'talk', I innocently ventured. The leaves were already turning brown and gold. The twists and turns of the path seemed, and perhaps were, endless. Perhaps, as Nanny Ritchie had hinted, the Maze had no centre and no way out. Soon I was lost, and a feeling came over me, enormous, indescribable, in which, in their different styles, could be traced all the traditions of English Gothic horror, romantic anguish and hopeless day-dreaming, passing rapidly away, galloping like cloudy horses into a darkening sky and leaving behind only the one question: Who am I?

Who, indeed? I was born on 19 April 1913, not at Wharton, but at a small, respectable house in a respectable road in a respectable part of Shipley in the West Riding, a mill town which was to become part of 'Greater Bradford'. I remember nothing of our neighbours. There was something which made us different from them. I and my brother and sister, the one ten years, the other seven years older than myself, were the fruit of a double exogamy.

My father, Paul Sigismund Nathan, was a younger son of Bernhard Nathan and Henrietta Seemann, of Magdeburg in Germany. They had emigrated to England in the 1860s to become part of the influential foreign element, mostly German, which did a great deal to advance the Bradford wool trade. My grandfather was half Jewish, half German; my grandmother also had Jewish blood, in what proportion I cannot say, because nobody ever told me and I have never found out. But neither of them was a practising Jew (nor, I believe, was either of their own parents). My grandfather was said, soon after they settled in Bradford, to have driven the visiting rabbi with imprecations from his door; my grandmother was positively anti-semitic, I believe: at any rate she was so anxious to disavow any Jewish antecedents that she made sure that none of her children, three sons and two daughters, married people with Jewish blood.

They lived in a large, gloomy house with a gloomy, shrubbery-infested garden, called 'Oakleigh', a magnate's house, a few miles away from us by tramline, in Manningham, then a superior part of Bradford where such people as the Rothensteins and Eurichs lived and Delius was born. They had several servants and a German governess from Upper Silesia who was called simply 'Fraülein' and, as far as I knew or know, had no other name. She was a peasant, simple, kindly, hard-working, making no distinction between English people, who were all strange to her in their various ways. Her English was not good; nor did it ever get better, as my grandparents habitually spoke German among themselves and their children were bilingual. After my grandparents died in 1928 and 'Oakleigh' was sold, she returned to Silesia and may, a poor old woman, have lived long enough to cry 'Heil Hitler!' and later be driven from her home, raped, slaughtered or all in turn by the advancing Red Army and its Polish supporters, bent on blind revenge.

Where and in what circumstances my father met my mother

round about the turn of the century I cannot say. But I can imagine the loud Germanic ructions which must have ensued in the gloomy halls of 'Oakleigh', particularly in the fabled 'morning-room' with its glass-fronted bookcase of brown-bound German classics and engraving of Böcklin's 'Toten-insel' on the wall, when their acquaintance became known to his 'Pater' and 'Mater', as he called them with some fear and trembling.

My mother, Bertha Wharton, was born at Gomersal near Mirfield in the West Riding, one of a large family belonging to the lowest fringes of the lower middle or small shop-keeping class. My maternal grandparents are no more than shadows to me: my grandfather, Charles, only a dim, bearded face with a melancholy look, in a yellowing photograph on the mantelpiece of the 'front room' of their terraced house somewhere in Bradford; my grandmother not even that. After my mother married into a world entirely strange to her and them in terms of class, race and money, she must, of necessity if not by choice, have moved away from them. I doubt if my mother's parents, or their other surviving children, Joe, Herbert, Percy and Gertrude, ever met my father's parents. If they did, my grandfather, a kind and, within his old-fashioned limits, rather easy-going man, would have received them with decent courtesy; my grandmother, sharp-tongued and snobbish, would not.

To judge from her photograph my mother was a small, well-rounded, dark-haired, very pretty Yorkshire girl, whose attraction for my father is obvious enough. It is possible that they 'had to be married'. Whether this was so or not, my father's marriage immediately distanced him from the rest of his family and their friends and thereby distanced my brother, my sister and myself. We became outsiders to people who were themselves outsiders.

I have vague memories of compulsory Sunday luncheon at 'Oakleigh', of the uncomfortable atmosphere in that place of fabled splendour close to the gates of Lister Park, with its big, soot-blackened garden and croquet lawn. My mother complained that her parents-in-law sometimes spoke German between themselves at table, perhaps in order to make adverse comments on her. There was certainly an unspoken assumption that a mistake had been made. My father, unlike his sisters, who made 'good' marriages into the English middle class, one to a Holmes, a member of an important wool family, the other to an Ambler, land agent to Lord Scarbrough, was continuously made aware of this; though there was no doubt one mitigating factor in my German grandmother's eyes: at least her foolish son had married a Gentile.

My mother, whose first-born, a boy, arrived in 1903, was Board School-educated, unlettered, almost illiterate. She now found herself visiting France and Switzerland. Her comment, made in her strong native accents, on the Alpine scenery, 'It's just like Todmorden', was received by my German grandmother with malicious satisfaction and endlessly retailed among her circle.

My mother stayed with my father, on his business trips in the prosperous reign of King Edward, at the best hotels in Paris, Madrid, Berlin; she even went with him to Buenos Aires. Everywhere she remarked on the oddity of all foreigners, the insolence of Spaniards, the fatuously small hats of Frenchmen. For her those were days of ambiguous glory. It might be thought that my father would 'raise her to his level', as the saying used to be. But in fact he had no level to raise her to but that of money, expensive clothes, 'champagne wine', asparagus, hand-made chocolates, Havana cigars and coloured bathsalts in huge glass jars. He was, by birth, a stranger himself; she, as a native Englishwoman, had her own kind of superiority.

He was a weak and amiable man of suppressed charm and humour. Though fluent in four languages, he spoke them all with a Yorkshire accent. He had no interest in books, art or even in his parents' German music, except of the most elementary kind. What happened was that rather than raising his young wife to his own 'social level', he tended to decline to hers. This he did in a certain masochistic spirit very characteristic of him. The more he felt the disapproval of his parents, the broader grew his West Riding accent. At the same time he introduced German words into his own growing family's vocabulary, which turned on my mother's lips into what I now know were amazing distortions but then seemed only a puzzling element in daily life. In effect they both lost their levels and we, their children, never had any. Here lay the source of much anger, much disruption, much misunderstanding, much bewilderment and strangeness. We had never heard of 'alienation'. But had some wandering psychologist climbed down from the clouds he would have rubbed his hands and eagerly reached for a new notebook.

There was one exception to the unspoken rule which virtually excluded my mother's family from our own. This was her younger sister Gertrude. She was a plain woman without hope of marriage, what was then called 'simple'. She had a small collection of books – a prayer book, a Bible, a herbal, a few late Victorian bestsellers like *A Peep Behind the Scenes*, *Froggie's Little Brother*, Marie Corelli's *Sorrows of Satan* and *The Master Christian*. She was addicted to 'Extra Strong Mint Imperials'. She could play simple hymn tunes on our out-of-tune upright piano. And she could work. Gradually she became incorporated into her sister's household as a kind of serf, butt of incessant jokes from my father and the elder children which she took uncomplainingly except for occasional outbursts of futile anger. She lost her own name and became known simply as 'Aunt', even referring to herself by this name and writing it in the flyleaves of her precious books.

She was an indifferent cook, whose rock buns and Eccles cakes were notorious for their leaden quality; her rice-pudding and bread were indistinguishable and her tea was disliked because she often forgot to put any in the tea-pot. But she was a great hand with the mangle, the bed-making, the dusting and the carpet-sweeping, and

7

carried out all tasks which her elder sister set her as well as she knew how.

There was nothing particularly good about her except her almost infinite patience, but there was nothing at all bad about her either. She was a holy innocent and as she was more in evidence and more indispensable in my own childhood than in the growing time of my much older brother and sister, she became, in a curious way, a strong influence in my life.

She was there, no doubt, at the scene of my earliest memory, the beach of St Anne's-on-Sea, where, when I was about two, we spent a wartime holiday. She was there in 1916, when my grandmother held in her hand the telegram from the War Office which announced that my uncle Percy, a private in the West Yorkshire Regiment, was missing on the Somme. She was certainly *not* there when a similar telegram arrived to announce the same news of my paternal uncle, my father's youngest brother Leo, a second lieutenant in the same regiment, to say nothing of the fate of various unknown relations who must have fallen in the German army.

Her strange locutions ('Gnaw's Zark', 'indegredients', 'lozenger' and 'galosher' – back-formations from the plural – are examples) and individual phonetic system may have had something to do with my early interest in words. She extended and elaborated the West Riding practice of using voiced sounds where standard English has unvoiced ('buz' for 'bus', 'uz' for 'us') in the most amazing way; and systematically interchanged plosive, fricative and velar sounds. She not only called me 'Mytle' and said 'goddles' for 'goggles' and 'rackle' for 'rattle' but even 'sithers' for 'scissors'.

Meanwhile, in other realms, great events were going on, no less than the transformation of the world. But they scarcely affected me. By the end of the Great War I was five years old. I can date an early memory to 1917, when I sat quietly looking at the pictures in the *Chatterbox Annual* for that year as the German Zeppelin which had been trying to bomb Hull passed harmlessly over Bradford (my mother, who was already beginning to be resentful of her strange situation and to hit back, said there were so many Germans in the city that the enemy naturally let it alone). I can date another memory precisely to 11 November 1918, when I waved a small Union Jack among crowds cheering our victory. Among the voices which resound from that period, all in the ponderous accents of the West Riding, are some which say 'Ireland? There's only one thing to do with it. They want to tow it out into the middle of the Atlantic and sink it', and others which say 'I'll tell you one thing. In t'next war we'll be fighting the French; they're nothing but a nuisance and always have been.' When there was talk of the League of Nations and the 'war to end war' my mother invariably said: 'There'll always be wars.' Nor, as far as I know, did anyone dissent from this opinion.

As the youngest child, I was thoroughly spoiled and something of a milksop. I cannot remember playing with other children. I doubt whether my brother and sister, though less spoiled than I was, played with any either. My parents, partly because of their peculiar position in life, partly because of the way this must have affected their attitudes to other people whether they knew it or not, seemed to have few if any friends whose children their own children might have played with. We were cut off from our cousins on my father's side, who were of roughly the same age, by snobbery on the one hand and by my mother's resentment and distrust on the other. As for the neighbours' children, my mother's general attitude may be summed up in the phrase 'You never know where they've been'.

Even our surroundings seemed – or so I think now – to reinforce the feeling of not belonging anywhere. There were parts of Shipley which were neither town nor country. There was a functioning farm, with real cows and sheep, among new-built villas. Sandy tracks led from abandoned mills, where mist rose from green-scummed mill-ponds, to wooded hollows where sour streams ran down past rows of terraced houses to the River Aire. A long steep path between high walls led to an empty villa in an overgrown garden, called the 'murder house', though nobody would ever tell me why. Near a collapsing hen-house in Nab Wood was a small, scrawny grove of trees. One particular hollow tree stump was invested with mystery. It contained secret messages, I believed, though I could never find them. This was my first intimation of the numinous, a momentary sense of awe and mystery, indescribably delicious. Not far away, at Cottingley Bridge, was the place where Sir Oliver Lodge, the once famous scientist, photographed the last fairies to be seen and the first to be photographed in England.

Further off, approached by a perilous railway-crossing ('don't forget to look both ways,' my mother and 'Aunt' always said in unison) was Shipley Glen, with its gas-tram and ginger beer in those bottles with glass marbles in the top which are now to be found only in the downstairs lavatories of modish publishers. I was not, of course, allowed to go to these places by myself. If I was not with my brother and sister, 'Aunt' would go with me, wearing her 'helmet' hat and one of the two 'costumes', one in 'nigger brown', one in 'navy blue', which she invariably wore. These, like most things about 'Aunt', were family jokes (there is nothing like a state of siege to encourage such cruel behaviour). While on our walks she would keep a look out for the herbs she had painfully read about in her herbal, particularly comfrey, which, she maintained, 'cured everything'. I cannot remember that she ever found any. This was another running joke.

So, as a family, we drew together in uneasy alliance, if it could be called that when our parents' almost continuous quarrelling and bickering (or 'fratching', as it was called) was becoming a part of daily life. This is not to say that my father and mother were not fond of each other in their own way. They were deeply attached. The idea of infidelity, if not unthinkable – there had once been a Miss Litchfield, governess to my brother and sister, who, it was whispered, 'had to go' – was certainly an idea only. And of course there were happy times amid the 'fratching'. It was in 1919, I think, that we first spent a holiday at Arncliffe, then a remote village in a remote part of the Yorkshire Dales, reached by pony-and-trap on a rough, stony road from the nearest station, Grassington, on the now long-abandoned branch-line from Skipton.

We stayed at first in The Falcon Inn, later in holiday cottages. Every day, if the weather was fine enough, we took our tea to a certain place on the left bank of the River Skirfare, where the water ran swiftly among limestone boulders, forming little beaches and pools for paddling which were deep enough for mild adventure but perfectly safe. Sometimes my father and brother went shooting the rabbits which lived in thousands on the limestone hills. My sister learned to ride a pony. I learned nothing except to keep quiet and observe the behaviour of others. Because of my silence, my German grandfather had nicknamed me 'Moltke', after the famous general who seldom spoke and was said to have smiled only twice in all his life. Because of my solemnity a business acquaintance (perhaps even a rare friend) of my father called me 'Canon Fletcher', after a local clergyman notable for his serious mien. Even 'Aunt' commented that I 'liked to sit'.

My parents, though they had been baptised into the Church of England and my mother had been confirmed, showed no interest in religion, apart from having their own children baptised at St Peter's Church in Shipley, on the uphill road that led to the ogre's wood. 'Aunt' occasionally went to church and once, when she had been goaded by my father's jokes about her gloves, rock-cakes or habit of reading Zadkiel's *Guide to Palmistry* (another volume in her small personal library) upside down, accused him of being an 'atheest'. My mother also pronounced the word in this unusual way.

Whether as Moltke, Canon Fletcher or mother's boy, I already began to show signs of habitual melancholy and of a certain torpor, an inability to take a normal, active interest in life which, had my parents been less conventional (within their unconventional situation), more imaginative or even more plain sensible, would have worried them more than it did. There are certain people who are born old. Hardy's 'Old Father Time', the child who hanged his half-brothers and sisters and himself out of despair and a conviction, shared with his creator, of the uncaring cruelty of the universe, is no myth. I know this because as a child I sometimes felt like that myself. At the age of eight I vowed to myself, after due consideration, not to commit suicide right away but to do so when my mother died. She was the only being, apart, perhaps, from my sister, whom I loved. She lived to be ninety-seven. I have not kept that vow.

Born to function, as it were, on one cylinder only, I had to make that one cylinder work overtime. I was much more intelligent than my parents or my brother and sister; I had a precocious fondness for words. Although I did not go to school until I was seven (my mother had somehow convinced herself that I was too delicate or sensitive, though there was no particular evidence of this delicacy except a dislike of games rougher than tig, pat-ball, snap or beggar-my-neighbour), I had already taught myself to read and even write after a fashion. I invented stories and histories of the dynasties of our dogs and cats. A little later I began writing plays in which our few friends or acquaintances appeared as grotesques. So began or first appeared a lifelong addiction to fantasy.

I have mentioned my first remembered experience of the numinous, the mysterious tree stump in Nab Wood. As time went on this indescribable feeling, one of intense pleasure, came to be attached to other features of the neighbourhood – a clump of trees on a ridge against the skyline on the road to a fabulous region, 'Chellow Dene', I had heard mentioned but never visited; a soot-black mill seen against the sunset; the movement of leafless boughs in Lister Park in winter; the sham stained glass in the fanlight of our front doorway. By sitting on the stairs and looking through this I could change the outer world at will into various forms of coloured illusion. Soon this feeling of disembodied ecstasy would visit me without apparent reason. I looked and hoped for its inexplicable onset and the few seconds it lasted – though perhaps it could not be measured in time, being outside it. I had another occasional sensation, neither pleasant nor unpleasant, but also, in its way, one of disembodiment. Lying stretched out on my back in bed before getting up in the morning I would suddenly feel that I was made of stone and of gigantic size. The sensation lasted only a few seconds and I felt it only over a short period of what must be called my childhood. I have never felt it since.

My first school was the kindergarten department of the Bradford Girls' Grammar School (my brother and sister were already pupils at the respective senior establishments). I remember nothing about this except the arrival of my first short school report. 'His application and ability to learn are excellent. But he is too passive and lacks initiative.' After my father had consulted his dictionary, one of the few books in the house apart from my fairy tales, my brother's and sister's adventure stories and 'Aunt's' personal library, there was a long discussion leading to a blazing row in which my mother condemned the teacher who had written this report in unmeasured terms and even talked of 'having it out with her', while my father, after accusing her of 'spoiling the child', slammed the door and cut off the rest of the conversation from my calm, impartial listening ears.

Later I went to the Junior Department of the Bradford Grammar School proper, a malodorous place smelling of ink, sweat and, faintly, of horses, in Fountain Street (I liked the name) in the central part of Bradford near the main school, a soot-black, towered building opposite the Yorkshire Penny Bank at the junction of steep, tram-groaning Cheapside and Darley Street which I was to know well later on. I remember nothing much about this junior school except bursting into tears in a 'nature study' lesson, losing my first brief fight (with a disagreeable Jewish boy I had tripped up on an irresistible impulse) rather ignominiously, and being called for at the end of school one afternoon by my father in a taxi, a cause of awe among my fellow-pupils, who were almost all of a class which did not take taxis. Normally, of course, I was taken to school on the tram by 'Aunt' and taken home by her. I dare say this was the cause not of awe but of derision among my fellows. I made no friends during the short time I was there.

A change now came over my family's fortunes. My father, though no 'hard man who looked as if he had done well out of the War', had shared, perhaps more by luck than good management, in the boom in the wool trade. So we moved from comparatively humble Shipley to proud Harrogate, where the rich people lived. Our new home, a large, irregularly-shaped villa portentously called 'Duchy Grange', had been built about the beginning of the century and so was old enough to have partly ivied walls. It had a terrace, lawn, winding paths, flower-beds, a big kitchen garden and a garage, though we had no car, still in 1920 the perquisite of the very rich and fashionable.

Already averse to change, I did not like the move, even though it was so obviously for the better. But my parents did. For a time they were much preoccupied with moving in and beautifying their new home with a fine big Persian carpet for the drawing-room, Dresden figurines, standard lamps, engraved steel fenders and other expensive objects of hideous art nouveau design, as well as Chippendale chairs and a splendid mahogany dining-room table with a sheet of heavy plate glass to cover it. Canteens of heavy silver appeared and a fine pair of Georgian silver candlesticks (pronounced Georgeéan by my mother) as well as hundreds of elaborate appliances such as card tables with inbuilt ashtrays and hinged rings for glasses.

Cards, which then meant 'auction bridge', were an important

preoccupation in the evenings when some of my parents' scarce friends came in for a few rubbers. My mother, unfortunately, was very bad at the game. Even though my father, who was reasonably good at it, was not, of course, partnering her, he still flew into the astounding rages which were becoming habitual, rising from the table to bang his head on the wall in only nominal mock despair, shouting at my mother in German and getting xenophobic shouts in return. I have abhorred bridge ever since, though I am fond of card games in general.

We had two servants, a cook and a housemaid. But my mother could not or would not maintain her new social status, now moved one notch higher. She would not trust the servants to carry out their duties and was for ever interfering with them, convinced, perhaps rightly, that she could do better herself. But whenever my father found her dusting, carpet-sweeping, cooking or, worst of all, washing up he would fall into one of his more and more frequent rages.

He travelled by train to Bradford most days to work in what was mysteriously called 'the Warehouse'. When he returned to his uneasy mansion in the evenings, irritated perhaps by racing losses (he was becoming an inveterate gambler) or faced with the worry of a housemaid's pregnancy, my mother would exclaim 'Here comes the Fleyboggard!' – a West Riding bogey – so as to get the children on her side. This often led to another blazing exogamic row.

At the same time my mother, angered by the Nathans, was beginning to brood more and more about her own family, the Whartons. A shadowy greatness gathered. She hinted and more than hinted at connections with the Whartons of Wharton Hall in Westmorland. For two hundred years they had been one of the greatest and most powerful families of the North. Their last, foolish, drunken head, Philip Wharton, had been created Duke, squandered his fortune, turned Jacobite and Catholic and fought with the Spaniards against his own countrymen at the Siege of Gibraltar, forfeiting title and estates and perishing miserably, to be commemorated by Pope in a famous passage of vitriolic eloquence: 'Wharton, the scorn and wonder of our days . . .' I don't think my mother had ever heard of Pope. But encouraged by my brother, who was interested in heraldry as well as golf and stamp-collecting, she took to remembering how her father was said to have come to Yorkshire from Westmorland as a child. She even hinted at a Missing Will. I listened and pondered.

One of the results of our move to genteel Harrogate, where 'nice people' lived and there were expensive shops for the adornment of my mother with fine clothes and enormous emeralds, was that my brother and sister were removed from their respective Bradford grammar schools and sent, not to English public schools like their cousins, but to schools in Switzerland, by the Lake of Geneva, where they mingled or at least met with other scions of the rich manufacturing class and also exotic foreigners, often Argentine. The general idea was that they should learn manners and French. The latter would be an asset for my brother when in due course he entered the wool trade.

As for me, I was the clever one. I was intended for public school and so was sent at the age of nine, in the first place as a day boy, to a prep school not more than half a mile from our house. Not liking the prospect, I arranged to get acute appendicitis just before my first term was due to begin in September 1921. I was rushed to a nursing home (there was no lack of them in Harrogate) and operated on, then tended by a pretty nurse with whom I fell in love, my first experience in that line.

My status as 'delicate' established to my mother's satisfaction, I enjoyed a prolonged convalescence. On the advice of the good Dr Nimmo-Watson, once a noted enthusiast for lemon juice, my mother took me to Brighton for a fortnight. I felt an access of the numinous, still faintly remembered now, amid the strange sea smells. Then we went to London, where we stayed at the then expensive and fashionable Piccadilly Hotel and were joined by my father, who had been on one of his business trips to Leipzig or Barcelona. My parents, for all I have said so unkindly about them, were fond of each other in their way. Their reunion gave me what may have been my first experience of jealousy. But in the reserved first-class carriage of the train which took us back to Harrogate, as the telephone wires dipped and rose past the windows and the big advertisements for Carter's Paints appeared rhythmically in the fields, they soon took to quarrelling again.

The quarrel may have been about a new pregnant housemaid or the jobbing gardener, a dour Yorkshireman called Lund. His bill was thought excessive, including as it did the wages of his assistant, the boy Norman. As a final move in a bitter campaign, Lund sent in a long, indignant letter. The concluding section of this began: 'And now as to Norman . . .'

This became a catch-phrase. It was a peculiarity of my family, particularly my father, to seize on such things as this and make them into the stock family jokes, quite unintelligible to other people, which relieved our endless dilemma of exclusion and rejection. My father had only to enter a room, pronounce the word 'Lund!' or 'Jessica Mumby!' (a particularly awkward, owlish, bespectacled housemaid) or 'Mrs Wertheimer!' (a bridge-playing neighbour who was suspected of cheating and figured as a grotesque mass murderess in one of my satirical melodramas) to bring the house down.

My mother, who had no sense of humour, was vaguely puzzled by these formulae which contained a world of comic meaning for the initiated. But they must have had something to do with the emergence in myself of that 'sense of humour' which, though it has helped, against all the odds, to keep me alive and even to earn me a living, is not a thing I can really approve of. There was cruelty in it. It reduced Lund, Jessica Mumby, Mrs Wertheimer and, amid a growing collection of such figures, several of the inhabitants of

Arncliffe, where in spite of our new grandeur we still spent all our holidays, to mere things, comic cut-outs with no claim to humanity. The putative psychologist would have been interested. He might even have made a note: 'defensive hysteria'.

'Aunt', who soon joined the Harrogate household as an all-purpose serf, was of course a primary character in this strange shooting-gallery. So were others of my mother's relations, particularly Aunt Annie, who lived with her husband, Uncle Herbert, in a terraced house in Manchester. He was a clerk, I think, a man of no particular note, humble, God-fearing, providing little or nothing for stock-jokery. Aunt Annie provided plenty. Troubled by constipation, she was said to resort to a legendary 'black draught' of prodigious power and was therefore known to my father as 'Black Draught Annie'. So 'Black Draught Annie!' or better still, 'Jallop!', a horse-drench said to be the main ingredient in the draught, became one of those key locutions and signals for general merriment.

My father himself took a keen interest in his bowel movements. Sometimes, when he had had a particularly satisfying one, he would announce the fact for all to hear. This growing 'vulgarity' was, I think, a form of defiance of his parents and of the superior social pretensions of his brothers and sisters, of whom we saw little even after our translation to Harrogate. It was part of a delight he had in self-abasement. He encouraged my brother, now back from Switzerland, to join him in these intestinal interests. Their farting competitions, I remember, were a feature of a motor tour we made one summer in a chauffeur-driven Daimler to the Scottish Highlands. Together with billiards, card-games and ritual pronouncements of 'Lund!' or 'Mrs Wertheimer!', they must have been, though deprecated by my mother, a relief from the incessant rain and misunderstandings about hotel-bookings.

At Strathpeffer a particularly spectacular farting competition – a fastidious observer, I took no part in such things – almost got us expelled from our gloomy hydro. At Braemar I became fascinated by the labyrinthine passages of the Invercauld Arms – material for many a pleasurable nightmare ever since – and for a time was pronounced 'lost'. Did I wish I had been? I am not sure.

The family 'sense of humour' stood me in good stead when the dreaded time arrived for me to join my prep school, Belgrave House. It was a curious kind of school in some ways. It was run, for a start, not by a headmaster but by two sisters, the Misses Nightingale, whose deputy-head, Mr Routledge, supplied the ogre figure of games-crazed disciplinarian I had been particularly dreading. He took an immediate dislike to me. By a strange chance, he died suddenly and most unexpectedly (he was about thirty, I suppose) of a heart-attack, not long after I joined the school. I was delighted.

Apart from my sense of humour, my main asset, if it was one, was a precocious intelligence. Excused games and gym in my first term because of delicacy, I shortly found I was exceptionally bad at both and though taking part half-heartedly in cricket and football, able to do somersaults of formal elegance and climb wall-bars as fast as anybody else, I was soon given up as hopeless. As for learning, although there were no books at home apart from bestselling novels (*Peter Jackson: Cigar Merchant*, *Blood and Sand* by Blasco Ibañez, the works of Sheila Kaye-Smith and Edgar Wallace) I soon got hold of some for myself and by the age of ten was probably as academically advanced as most of the teachers at Belgrave House, none of whom had university degrees. But the geography master, an amiable young idiot, had a sports car, and the English master, who practised sarcasm in a big way, once made the fearful prediction that I should live to be editor of *Punch*.

Another occasional teacher was Percival Hale Coke, a drawling, languid man with a monocle, who wore a pork-pie hat and was a local poet and man of letters. I was a pretty-looking boy and he took a special interest in me. He was sympathetic, for instance, as well as intrigued when, one autumn evening during a scripture lesson, he handed me a box of matches and asked me to stand on my desk and light the gas. Alas! I had led a life so sheltered that I did not know how to strike a match! His monocle fell from his eye and he looked, as he often did, most quizzical.

Perhaps to smooth over the contretemps, as well as out of interest, he said, in his slow drawl and 'upper-class' lisp, 'But why are you in this lesson anyhow? Aren't you Jewish?' 'He is by rights,' said a big, forthright boy, Theakston, perhaps, the brewer's son, in a reasonable, tolerant sort of way. I cannot remember what I said. Nothing, perhaps. Already conscious of so many differences between myself and others, I did not think of this dubious one as particularly important. It was not talked about at home, where the Vicar of St Wilfrid's, the big, rich Victorian parish church, was an occasional baffled visitor.

After a time, to make me more fit to stand up to public school, I became a boarder, though only a weekly one. It was my 'sense of humour' that got me through the mild bullying, the games, the crocodile walks, the toothpaste or wet knotted towel tortures and other conventional features of prep school life even in this peculiar and rather crummy specimen. There were even moments of enjoyment – one in particular on a summer evening after cricket when, for no reason at all, I suddenly felt for a moment that I was redeemed from singularity and an accepted member of the human race. It passed, but the feeling seems significant even now – an earnest of what might with luck and insight have been nourished and made habitual; even as things fell out, it stands as a pledge of something which cannot be destroyed.

Apart from my 'sense of humour' my intelligence helped. I found learning absurdly easy and was avid for knowledge. Finding among my brother's books (he also had his singularities, as will appear) Sir Wallis Budge's text and translation of the Egyptian Book of the

Dead, I became fascinated by the hieroglyphs and resolved to master them. I even persuaded my mother to take out a subscription for me to the *British Journal of Egyptology*. Suddenly, growing afraid of that cold, huge, monumental civilisation – was it the source of my own stony sensations? – I lost interest, declared myself, self-consciously and in due form, freed from the 'bondage of the Egyptians' – and switched to Assyriology and cuneiform. Would I have gone on to Aztec if more conventional studies had not intervened?

I can remember making only one friend at this school, if you could call him a friend rather than an acolyte. He was a small, fat, idle, rather stupid, dark-haired boy called Haigh; and for a time was my constant companion or attendant. 'I can't make out what you see in him,' said the English master in a friendly way. What did I see in him? Subservience, perhaps. To be most at ease with inferiors – or supposed inferiors – is not uncommon with those who lack assurance. But perhaps there was something else in Haigh that made him interesting to me. He left the school before I did. I wonder whether he was the same Haigh – the physical features certainly correspond – who thirty years later was to make his mark in the world as the murderer of Mrs Durand-Deacon at the Onslow Court Hotel?

The time was now approaching when I was due to sit for a scholarship at a public school. I doubt if such a scholarship, even of the humblest kind, had ever been won by a pupil of Belgrave House in all its history, but in my case Winchester was the first school suggested. I was to have special tuition in Greek! Immense excitement seized me. Long before my first lesson with the sallow, strange-faced Mr Pereira, notorious for his bad breath and unpopularity with the other masters, I had learned the Greek alphabet, could decline the present tense of 'luo' and had a considerable vocabulary.

All the same I did not succeed in winning a scholarship either at

Winchester or at Shrewsbury, where my eldest cousin, son of my father's bossy elder sister Gertrude Ambler (the antithesis of 'Aunt'), who was particularly fond of squashing my mother, had been some years before, later proceeding to Oxford. What was the reason? 'He is too passive and lacks initiative'?

This was the time when our family fortunes began to collapse. The climax of our fortunes must have been that Christmas when on three successive nights, my father and his two sisters and their families entertained each other in turn, vying in their hospitality. Aunt Gertrude Ambler, whose husband had disappeared mysteriously from the scene, now lived at 'Oakleigh' itself. She had lost her independent base at Stone Grange – a real grange on Lord Scarbrough's estate at Sandbeck near Roche Abbey, and to me a place of romance and mystery – and was only marginally an Ambler. But this did not prevent her from eyeing our arrangements at 'Duchy Grange' with a patronising eye or criticising my mother's hospitality as crushingly as she could manage. We were still made to know our place.

One exotic at these celebrations was Irene, whom my tiny uncle Julius, a judge in Malaya, was said to have met on board ship, and, after an attack of infatuation, married. She had been a youngish widow, with dark good looks, suspected of being both a 'siren' and an 'adventuress'. She was certainly accustomed to more sophisticated company than the Nathans or even the Holmeses (though not necessarily the central Amblers) and so though less respectable, had an advantage over my overbearing Aunt Gertrude or my sharp-tongued Aunt Marian.

She was shingled, could Charleston and shimmy, used a long diamond-encrusted cigarette-holder and could manage some fashionable small-talk. She embarrassed my brother, then approaching his majority, fascinated my sister, now in her late teens, and took, or affected to take, a great interest in myself, both for my prettiness and my mimetic talents ('he'll sit there saying nothing and taking it all in,' my mother would explain, 'and then, when you've gone, he'll do a perfect imitation of you'). Irene said she would like to adopt me. But the offer, serious or not, was declined.

That Christmas, with its round of hospitality, was the bright end of the old order. The slump was on its way. My grandfather lost money; my father, with less to lose, bad at managing his affairs and with a growing addiction to gambling and other kinds of extravagance, of which expensive chocolates from Charbonnel and Walker were only a symbol, was not exactly ruined but was certainly brought down in the world. 'Duchy Grange' was sold amid violent recriminations, and we moved to a tall semi-detached house, servantless except for 'Aunt', in a less select part of Harrogate.

A little after this my sister, who had begun to have a reputation for being 'fast', asserted her independence and after furious rows and accusations, made her escape. She had become a great dog-lover, was given a beautiful Irish setter for her twenty-first birthday and through this became fast friends with a formidable lady Alsatian-breeder, a well-to-do scion of an ancient Scottish family, who had bought a derelict old water mill and other properties in a Dales village. With her my sister, breaking with my parents, took refuge in a canine paradise, shared with the dog-fancier's only son, who later married her. My brother was despatched to get my sister back, but failed in his mission. 'Words were said which could never be forgotten or forgiven.' My father, never one to assert himself, shrugged his shoulders hopelessly. 'Aunt' recommended comfrey. The atmosphere became sulphurous.

I overheard my mother and brother concocting a secret plan. They would leave my father, the Fleyboggard, take my mother's name of Wharton and, presumably with me in tow (or was Irene's offer still open?) settle in Bedford and, after selling my mother's jewellery, make an entirely fresh start. Why Bedford? I never knew.

In any case the scheme came to nothing. Soon afterwards my brother made his own escape, both from our strange family and from the collapsing wool trade.

His own way of escape was into sheep farming, first as an apprentice to a farmer in Upper Wharfedale and then as a shepherd in Waldendale, a tributary valley of Wensleydale and as remote a place as any in England. Has there ever been another shepherd in the Yorkshire Dales called Nathan who was educated at an expensive boarding school in Switzerland? He always sought out the most remote places he could find, and when he married a Swaledale girl and took a farm of his own it was high up among the wild moors at the head of that northern-most of the Yorkshire Dales, an isolated starvecrow place approached only by a boulder-strewn road, in winter a torrent. The domestic water supply came from a moorland stream bubbling into a rough stone basin.

Soon he became more of a Yorkshire dalesman than any ever born. He changed his modified West Riding accent for the more attractive North Riding one. He went to market, bought and sold, could talk of 'clipping' and dipping and cairds and ticks with the best. A lean, very energetic man with saturnine good looks, he spent his days alone with his flocks on the wild moors. He was probably the last sheep-farmer in England to wear clogs. He was also one of the last to cut and stack peat for fuel in the immemorial way. For all I know he may, in his lonely fanaticism, have counted his sheep by the old Celtic numerals he had read about in the countryside-crazed books of the Leeds topographer Edmund Bogg. He had a good wife, a genuine sheep-farmer's daughter, to share this hard, dedicated, yet in a typically Nathanian way, essentially make-believe existence. I do not think he made any friends among his fellow farmers, or wanted any.

Meanwhile, in Harrogate, life was changing for me. I had reached the troubled age of puberty with its half-understood and confused desires which I, a shy, withdrawn boy with no close friends of either sex, learned all too well to satisfy in secret after the customary fashion. Nobody told me the 'facts of life'. I found, hidden in a drawer in my parents' bedroom, a copy of *Married Love*, by Marie Stopes, wrapped in brown paper inscribed *My Travels in Canada*, by the Bishop of Birmingham, together with *The Picture of Dorian Gray*, similarly wrapped and inscribed *My Travels in Australia*, by the Bishop of Liverpool. But a hasty glance at both works merely confused me further.

With puberty came a loss of reasoning power and concentration, perhaps not unusual in very precocious children. There was now no hope of my going to a public school. It was decided that I should go to the Bradford Grammar School, travelling there and back by train every week-day, escorted to Harrogate station and back by 'Aunt'. I was now among a rougher sort of boys, some of whom mimicked my 'improved' Yorkshire accent and tended, though without malice, to set my hair on fire or interfere with my share of the appalling hash and custard served every day for lunch for boys who for various reasons did not go home for it. The meal was superintended by Mr Pallister, the head laboratory assistant, who with Sergeant Sugden, the dreaded gym instructor, formed the NCO element of the staff. The school was divided into five departments, Classics, Mathematics, Science, History and Modern Languages. Classics, to which I adhered, was acknowledged, though grudgingly by some, to be by far the most respected discipline. The headmaster, Dr Edwards, like many of the masters a Welshman, occasionally took classical periods himself. He was a fussy, rather weak man with a walrus moustache, not greatly respected except for his office.

I now found myself taught by masters very different from the drop-outs and farceurs of Belgrave House. Even the humblest was a graduate and my own shortcomings became more obvious. I usually had only a medium position in the various classes through which I passed, eventually to reach the Classical Sixth, the apex of the school, where Mr Lionel Pelling Lewis, a most remarkable Welshman, presided, with Mr Robertson, a lovable Irishman, as his second-in-command.

Mr Lewis had cultivated a schoolmaster's eccentricity to a point bordering on madness. A small, fierce-looking, bald, grey-bearded man who always wore a pale blue tie passed through a ring, he came rushing through the door to his desk without a pause, sat down, pinched his nose and cheeks and scratched his beard in a ritual manner, adjusted his gold-rimmed pince-nez and then shouted in a high, sharp, harsh voice like a demented parrot: 'Waterhouse!' or 'Sutcliffe!' or 'Murgatroyd!' or even 'Nathan!' – '*Prometheus Desmotes* – line 102 – construe!'

Should there be hesitation, his high-pitched 'next, next, next, next, next', uttered with extreme rapidity, had a paralysing effect. But sometimes he would rush to his desk at the beginning of a period and, without even alluding to the classics, recite, in the same harsh, absurdly mannered tone (a gift to schoolboy mimics – I can still do it without effort) 'The Hunting of the Snark' or other poems by Lewis Carroll.

But he was an excellent teacher with a true love of language. His methods were as eccentric as himself. To illustrate precisely the alternative uses of a Greek preposition he would make groups of boys stand at different levels, on benches, desks or even on top of a tall cupboard. Sometimes, during one of these noisy charades, the headmaster would put his head round the door, then withdraw it with a deprecating cough. A look of subtle, indescribable complicity passed between Mr Lewis and his class. They never forgot the uses of those prepositions.

I was an indifferent worker. But I soon became, even without Mr Lewis's influence, a lover of language, as in a childish way I had always been. It had been music which invaded my soul in the first fervour of adolescence. There was no music at home except for my sister's jazz records or my father's 'Liszt's Hungarian

Rhapsody No 2' – sole sad relic of his parents' standard German-Jewish culture. Brahms, my grandfather's favourite, was always said to be 'too heavy'. Now I began saving up my pocket money to buy records, progressing very rapidly from Ketèlbey's 'In a Persian Market' to Beethoven's Symphonies and Debussy's 'L'Après–midi d'un Faune', which I played ceaselessly on the big, mahogany cabinet wind-up gramophone which had somehow survived from 'Duchy Grange'.

Soon, poetry superseded music as my primary passion, though without supplanting it. Palgrave's *Golden Treasury* was always with me. I could repeat 'Lycidas' by heart. I began to write poetry myself, adolescent stuff with Keats as first model, then the earlier Yeats. It was sad stuff indeed. All the same I was beginning to learn how to write. I stood top of the class in English though in nothing else. As for maths, I was so hopeless, so unable to see 'what it was about' (nobody ever told me that it was not 'about' anything) that I had to have extra tuition in it to get me through Matriculation, an exam for which elementary maths was obligatory. That hurdle once passed, I never had to look seriously at a number again in all my days at school or university. Now, unable to do the simplest sum and almost incapable of abstract thought, though hopelessly fascinated by astronomy, I know what I have missed.

Games were not compulsory at the Bradford Grammar School. In my spare time I mooned about, read voraciously and at week-ends explored the pleasant, secluded country north-west of Harrogate in an obsessive way, tramping every lane and field-track in a romantic fervour. I had a fiercely protective feeling for these places, resentful of any change in them, whether pylon or metalled road or any other sign of 'progress' – a 'conservationist' before the time. Among those woods and foothills on the edge of the Pennine moors momentary experiences of the numinous were frequent and more intense than ever. Even the fact that 'Aunt', on my mother's insistence, had to go with me in case I should fall down a hole or be kidnapped by gypsies, did not spoil my ardour. A strange pair we must have looked as we walked the green lanes or ate our symbolic sandwiches under a beech tree – she vacant and silent with her unvarying 'helmet' hat and 'costume', I with wild black hair, repeating poems or gabbling a spell I had got out of Eliphas Levi's *Transcendental Magic*. I do not think I was very kind to her.

In 1929, when I was sixteen, still Aunt-ridden but consumed with music, poetry and ineffectual lust, there was a further decline in my father's fortunes. Bouts of 'fratching' had reached a new intensity after the escape of my brother and sister and their mutual estrangement. My father had become addicted to 'having a gastric ulcer', sometimes rolling on the floor and groaning in agony in a manner so theatrical that the poor man's genuine pains, augmented and perhaps originally produced by a sense of failure in life, got little or no sympathy. Even 'Aunt' told him not to be a baby. During one of these amazing exhibitions, our neurotic Aberdeen terrier, Bodo (named after Bodo von Elstein, a real person as well as a character in one of my satirical dramas, who once, looking back lasciviously at a pretty girl in the street, had fallen over a passing dog and broken his leg – a great family 'joke') – this unlucky animal began running round in circles, foaming at the mouth and 'encapsulating', as some might say, the strange lunacy of our lives.

When we moved from Harrogate to a semi-detached house in Nab Wood, not very far from where I was born, my mother, resentful of this decline, brooded more often on the Missing Will, the Wharton Inheritance and all that might have been. Now that 'Oakleigh' was gone and my father's remaining family, firmly part of the English middle class, ceased to have much connection with him, he became even more deliberately plebeian, acquiring furtive gambling associates in Bradford and wasting what remained of his inheritance on the horses. My mother's reproaches, for all the genuine affection they still had for each other in spite of the violent rows, had no effect. Her growing tendency to recall past days of grandeur, of rich hotels and foreign journeys, of fine clothes and jewellery and bathsalts, which grew ever grander in her confused recollection, did not help to keep the peace.

We now spent our holidays, including Christmas, on my brother's farm, Fell End, in Swaledale. As part of his sheep-farming character he had developed an exaggerated meanness, conscious and half-theatrical. He would go to a certain cupboard and return smoking a cigarette. Up on the moor he had a small personal coalmine – a mere hole in the ground, with a ladder, pickaxe and bucket. The coal it yielded was of wretched quality, but it cost nothing. So he insisted on using it for the grudgingly lit fire in the parlour, where it smouldered sulphurously, occasionally exploding and showering the room with fragments of shale and slate.

'If you want proper coal, you must bring your own,' he told my father. So it was a strange party which alighted from the bus, after the twenty mile journey from Richmond, at the end of the steep, rough track to Fell End. We staggered up the hill, burdened not only with chickens, potatoes and other kinds of food, as well as boxes of my father's favourite *marrons glacés*, the one feature of his luxurious past he could not bear to do without, but also with heavy sacks of coal, 'Aunt' and myself carrying one between us.

It was difficult for my father to slink away from Fell End to place bets. The nearest telephone was several miles away. His lust for gambling had to be assuaged by games of Parcheesi, a form of Ludo, for which he gave small prizes. The game became a passion, with me as with the rest. Great tournaments were organised – marathon sessions of a dozen games or more, in which even my brother sometimes joined, shaking the dice-box vigorously with his lean, hard, bony hand and moving the counters while an occasional sheep-tick fell upon the board. My father was a bad loser, not because of meanness – he was a very generous man – but because he was the butt of all the jokes that were going, throwing more than his share of 'three sixes' (which meant that your counter was sent back to base) to roars and screams of demented laughter. Once, teased beyond endurance, he seized the board, tore it to pieces and flung it on the fire, which immediately exploded, covering him with debris as he rolled on the floor in a positively blood-and-thunder demonstration of his gastric ulcer, while Bodo had another of his fits.

'Domimina Nustio Illumea,' said a voice one day as we assembled in the school hall for morning prayers. I saw a short but compact and muscular boy, or rather, young man, two or three years older than myself, with a pale, square face, dark copper-coloured hair and greenish-brown eyes. There was something very unusual in that face. To call it merely elfin or mischievous would not do justice to it. It was watchful and somehow not quite of this world. The words – which were, of course, simply produced by a horizontal reading of the school motto on its two-paged open book high up in the window behind the dais where the masters sat – made a strong impression on me, both solemn and absurd. As we sang the hymns – 'casting down their golden crowns upon the glassy sea' – the words chimed through my mind with magical effect. They corresponded exactly with my own love of all that was odd and strange.

This was the first time I met Alan Robertson Davis, to give him his full name. He was a noted, even famous figure in the school, a good classical scholar, already in the Sixth and preparing for university while I was still in the Remove or 'Transitus'. He was a wonderful speaker in the Debating Society. He was a member of the OTC. He was also a member of another kind of army. His father, now dead, and his mother and only sister all were or had been officers in the Salvation Army. Alan played a trombone in the band and spoke of the 'glory' of marching along in the rain through the slums of Bradford where the Army worked to feed the poor and bring sinners to the Mercy Seat. 'Glory' was a word which was often on his lips, and not only in that connection. He seemed always to be aware in a direct way, as I could only occasionally be, of the glory of the World and of the Word, and of worlds and words beyond these. One of his heroes was Rudolf Steiner, the founder of anthroposophy and of a discipline which could give experience of those other worlds. He was writing, as well as curious poems, a novel – 'the novel' – in which such unearthly matters were combined with fantastic absurdity.

Alan Davis – and we became friends immediately and remained so, with intermissions, for the rest of his short life – was the only man of undoubted genius I have ever known intimately. He was to be killed in action against the Japanese, an officer in the West Yorkshire Regiment, in the retreat from Burma in 1942. Had he lived he might have done great things, not necessarily as a writer, but in spheres I cannot even guess at. I say 'might', because there was, if we are thinking of worldly achievement even of the highest kind, a lack of effort in him, a drifting, a vagueness. It was as though he already belonged to another world and could not take this one seriously.

Meanwhile our friendship prospered. We were complementary to each other – he of Welsh and Scottish birth, entirely 'Celtic', I of curiously mixed origin but needing a focus for loyalties which I had already found in the dubiously 'Celtic' world of Yeats. Both devoted to languages, the more outlandish and useless the better, we studied Welsh, Irish and Scottish Gaelic together. He introduced me to the world of George Borrow's *Lavengro* – a whole enchanted realm of scholarship and adventure. We began to invent a private language on complex grammatical principles – its nouns, I remember, with their eleven cases and nine declensions, had not only a dual but a triune number.

We used to meet after school most days to drink cups of tea – alcohol was yet unthought of – in the steamy refreshment room

31

at the Midland Station in Forster Square, hard by the grand, marble-infested Midland Hotel, haunt of rich woolmen. There, in its 'French Restaurant', with its *flambé* fires suggesting, with the absurd incongruity I loved, Homeric sacrifices to the gods, my father occasionally treated me to a meal which to him must have suggested, most sadly, the glories of his past.

But that was a different world. In 'Fingal's Cave', as we called the station refreshment room because of its fluted pillars and dim, mysterious atmosphere, with a suggestion that the sea was breaking outside, we talked no end of wonderful nonsense. 'The Prometheus Club', a conspiratorial organisation dedicated to our particular kind of visionary enlightenment, was one project. As far as I know it never had more than two members. For the rest, there were Celtic matters, mingling incongruously with the elaborate mythology we were building out of the dark, rainy streets of Bradford itself: the great soot-blackened Victorian Gothic Town Hall with its bell-booming towers; Darley Street with its statue of the great Richard Oastler, noble-hearted Tory Radical; and its public reference library which we believed was haunted by the ghost of Edmund Bogg.

But all Bradford and its surroundings, half town, half country, had become magical, fulfilling those numinous intimations I had had from the beginning. There were giants in those days, enchanters in the decaying wool magnates' houses among the overgrown gardens and straggling groves. To ride on the groaning trams, jangling their earnest bells, was a majestic privilege, particularly when they took us to the far-off Cross Flatts Terminus, beyond Bingley, from which we could soon reach Ilkley moor. But the moor itself, though good for 'a health-giving walk', lacked the magical incongruity of Bradford itself.

It did not occur to me, or to my friend, to wonder what others made of our friendship. Very little, I imagine. It was totally innocent. Neither I nor any of the people I knew had ever heard of homosexuality, or if they had would not have dreamed of speaking of it, except in shocked hints when some wretched clergyman or cinema organist was mysteriously disgraced. We sometimes talked of girls, of those unimaginable goddesses we would one day love. Alan claimed to be in love with Olive, a tea-shop waitress, and even to have borrowed half-a-crown from her. But in such matters we were backward, in my case, at least, from shyness and a devotion to the ideal.

I never met Alan's mother and sister. To Alan, I suppose, brought up in strict and respectable poverty, my family must have seemed rich. He came to our house once or twice, making a good impression, and must have noticed the signs of wealth, though diminished, in its incongruous furnishings.

We had lives, of course, apart from each other. I had other friends among my contemporaries – mostly the middle-class members of my form who shared my interest in literature and 'intellectual' pursuits and my lack of interest in games, and may even have written poems as bad as my own or worse. But they are, by comparison, shadowy figures in my memory – Bell, Waterhouse, Preston, Pendlebury, Rushworth: what became of them? And making their way upwards in the school, though junior to me, were such pupils as Alan Bullock and Denis Healey, already bent, I dare say, on making a name for themselves in academic and public affairs. My own purposes were quite other. I thought nothing of such things then and think little enough of them now.

Alan Davis became head of the school and a very popular one. For all his peculiarities, neither the headmaster nor others in authority could ignore his outstanding qualities. He had also won an Open Classical Scholarship to Lincoln College, Oxford, and there he went in the Michaelmas Term of 1930, ending this short epoch in my life and leaving me somewhat disconsolate. I had now passed my Higher School Certificate Examination, with distinctions in Latin and English. It was the latter, I think, which won me a

West Riding County Major Scholarship, worth £50 per annum. I now set about working for a Classical Scholarship myself. Incited by the delights of Oxford life which Alan described in his letters and at our occasional meetings during his vacations and my holidays, I resolved to follow him, as he urged, to Lincoln.

Along with my coevals I travelled by train to Oxford several times in the university vacations to take the scholarship examinations of various groups of colleges, when we naive provincials stayed in undergraduates' empty rooms – the cause of wonder and envy. Those were strange journeys in a strange country – since my childhood I had scarcely ever been out of Yorkshire, and never in the south of England. I looked at Oxford and the flat countryside, with its sluggish streams, pollarded willows, neat woods and glimpses of ancient houses in parks still unravished – a kind of English life then near its end – with bewildered eyes.

On one of these visits – I cannot remember (or do not want to remember) in which college I was staying – I met an anti-semitic demonstration for the first time in my life. It was only a matter of a few drunken 'hearties', staying up, perhaps, for extra study in the vacation, invading my allotted set of rooms and braying a few insults. But I was no less shocked by this experience for being surprised and hardly knowing what to make of it. I did not think of myself as Jewish and was in fact no more than a quarter Jewish by race. I was angry and disturbed to have this label – by these English bullies so abhorred and despised – stuck on me willy-nilly. It made me think; not happily.

Meanwhile, though one by one my contemporaries were winning scholarships and exhibitions at various colleges, I made no progress. My mind, bemused by adolescent fantasies, was not working well. And perhaps there was another reason for repeated failures. I did not shine at the personal interviews. 'He is too passive and lacks initiative.' That was a bad time for me. My natural indolence and torpor had returned. For days on end I would moon about, stare

34

out of my window at Nab Wood with a blank mind, or slump in my chair, thinking of nothing, my books unread.

At the same time I had got into the habit of playing the fool in the school classes from which I should soon, had all gone well, have had the prospect of an honourable delivery as an undergraduate-to-be. I began writing a fantastic story about a novelist, Egbert Masterman, author of a puritan romance, *Billiards and Sin*. One day, while I was thus engaged in class, I received a stinging blow on the cheek from an exercise book. 'What are you doing?' roared the new young English master, scarcely older than myself, and evidently ignorant of my greatness. 'Writing a novel,' I explained. He sent me to the headmaster, who chided me in his mild manner. It was a low point in my schooldays.

At another time I grew a moustache and, seeing no reason to stop, a full beard. This made me, I believed, the only bearded schoolboy in the West Riding, perhaps in the British Isles. The headmaster, evidently thinking I should grow out of these idiot vagaries, did not trouble to reprimand me or order me to shave off my beard. In this he was wise. I soon decided it did not suit me, removed it and have never seriously grown one since. When a more eccentric and amiable young English master replaced my enemy, he found me writing odes in class and said: 'You aren't making much of these. You must be one of those writers who will be remembered only for a few divine fragments.'

In the spring of 1932 I was nineteen. There was now no hope of my winning a scholarship to university. But I must now leave school. What was to become of me? Unfitted for business or for any useful occupation, I was in the situation of the young Borrow – but without his prodigious energy, physical stamina and giant courage. It was my County Major Scholarship which saved me. I was offered a small supplement to it and my father agreed, out of his dwindling resources, to supply enough money for me to live at Oxford, barely but no worse than some. Lincoln College

35

agreed, on the score of my past work, to give me a place. And there in the Michaelmas Term of 1932 I went as a Commoner of Oxford University.

2
Whining and Dining

It was not, I suppose, until I went to Oxford and so, as far as such a thing is possible, escaped from my family as my brother and sister had done before me in their different ways, that I realised how extremely odd they all were. This realisation did not, of course, come all at once but gradually, as I met various people, both dons and undergraduates, who might be described as 'normal', with more or less 'normal' parents, with roots in life which they took for granted and a recognisable place in the world. The realisation that I was irredeemably odd myself and could not be otherwise, came later. The realisation that many if not all of these supposedly normal people were quite as odd, in their own perhaps less complicated ways, as my own parents and myself came later still; it is hard to grasp even now.

Being odd, I gravitated towards other out-of-the-ordinary people. Most, if not all, of the friends and close acquaintances I had at Oxford were out-of-the-ordinary. My initial attempts to 'fraternise' with the general run of undergraduates at Lincoln, who worked reasonably hard, rowed or played other games, generally met with rebuffs, for reasons which I did not care to analyse (my surname was obviously one of them). Once rebuffed, I did not try again. Once hurt, I would not risk another wound. I became expert at knowing exactly what things could be said to what people. So with most people I tended to be silent. I did not like this myself and the knowledge that most people did not like it either made my self-conscious agonies of silence even more painful.

The world I entered at Oxford was entirely different, I found (and here at least I was the same as others) from the world I had come from. I had often wondered what it would be like not to have been born Michael Nathan in the West Riding. It seemed inconceivable in those early days that there were any other places in England, let alone the world, where it would be possible to have been born. The very thought brought on a feeling of vertigo.

So I settled into my rooms at Lincoln that first autumn evening (they were on the top floor of the first staircase on the right as you passed through the porter's lodge), and arranged my few belongings, mostly books, amid the meagre furniture of my 'sitter' and 'bedder'. Why do I dislike these terms so much that I find it hard to write them? Why do I dislike writing 'the Corn', 'the High', 'the Broad', 'the House'? Why is it that whenever I visit Oxford now, the needle on the dial of my pocket angstometer flickers upwards? The reason will become clear.

I was very much alone that first term. My idol Alan Davis was the only person I knew from school. Lincoln was a small college, though ancient, and ranked rather low in the hierarchy of colleges in those days (it has come up in the world since), and most of my fellow Bradfordians (apart from those like my old friends Waterhouse, Bell, Rushworth, Preston and Pendlebury, who had, I think, all got scholarships or exhibitions at Cambridge) were at other, larger colleges. Many from the North, particularly from Yorkshire, were at the Queen's College. There was a legend, founded on fact, that they occupied the Back Quad there *en masse*, forming a sub-culture of their own. They retained their native accents unimpaired, followed the fortunes of Bradford City, Huddersfield or Leeds United and even had copies of the *Bradford Telegraph and Argus* sent to them in big bundles every week, reading them aloud to each other every Saturday evening when other undergraduates were getting drunk, at sessions which lasted far into the night. These strange creatures never left their college except to go to lectures. They would have been fair game for persecution by the public school boys who were then the majority of undergraduates had they not been both tough and incomprehensible, obstinate as toads. So they were left alone to their strange rituals.

Alan Davis, whose rooms, much larger and more pleasant, as befitted a Scholar, were below mine on the same staircase, took me under his wing. We went for walks in the Parks or to a strange hamlet, Woodeaton, which he had incorporated into his mythology. There was a shuttered, deserted manor-house in a neglected park and a small, ancient church which always seemed to have a bird trapped inside it. We could never release it for all our efforts. We climbed up perilous ladders to the birdlimed, spider-webbed belfry and once, by kicking, brought a sound, deep-toned and strange, from the single great bell. Our shared world of fantasy was still in being, a consolation to me in my general loneliness. But Alan was two years older than myself, he had already taken 'Honour Mods' (again that twinge), was an important figure in the life of the college and had friends of his own year who did not greatly take to me.

I remember very little of that first term except the melancholy feeling of Oxford in autumn: the drifting leaves in the cobbled lanes, the dank mists which rose from its two rivers, the sound of bells which filled the air on Sunday evenings. Sam, my 'scout', who made my bed, cleaned my rooms, brought my coal for the tiny fire and my lunchtime 'Commons' of bread and cheese, must have thought me a quiet, well-behaved person who would give him no trouble. He soon had reason to change that opinion. He was a ruddy-faced, rather sly Oxfordshire man who had once worked in a lunatic asylum and used to tell his fellow-scouts that most of the young gentlemen (of whom I was one by courtesy) were much the same as the inmates.

I read my books, went to the prescribed lectures, had weekly tutorials with the bursar, a bumbling, amiable man whose reading-room was always in a state of indescribable confusion. He took up a lot of time scrabbling vaguely among the mountainous masses of paper on his desk. I did not mind this. I was gradually sinking into a familiar state of torpor. I often felt, as I tried to read, in my rooms or in the Union library (I had joined the Union on Alan's recommendation), a pervading sense of unreality, accompanied by an aching of the joints. One evening towards the end of that first term I sat in the one meagre armchair in my room, devoid of thought or hope, with an uneaten slice of chocolate Swiss Roll on the table beside me. I had not even the energy or interest to light the fire or turn on the light. I may have spent an hour or so sitting there in the gathering dark when a fellow-undergraduate whom I hardly knew even by sight came in on some pretext. 'I say, are you all right? Don't you even want the light on?' 'No,' I said. 'I don't.' 'Are you sure you're all right?' 'No.' After a while he left, baffled and vaguely worried.

Then one evening – I think it was the last evening before the end of that first term – all was changed. I don't know quite how it was, but I found myself, after dining in hall and perhaps drinking more than my usual modest amount, milling about with a crowd of my fellows who were singing, shouting and joking inanely. Most likely I had made some joke, out of that latent 'sense of humour' of mine, which took their fancy. They were already drunk; accepted into their company, I became so. I discovered the pleasure of drinking. I rampaged about with the rest; played the fool; made friends who at the time seemed lifelong; was sick into somebody's fireplace; and at last staggered up my stairs to bed, to wake next morning with my first hangover, feeble enough, but a pleasant accompaniment for my new companions' talk of the extraordinary doings of the previous night. When, later that day, I boarded the train at Oxford Station en route for Bradford (change at Rugby) I had acquired a different view of the place.

My course was set. My career at Oxford (contrary to the high hopes of my parents and of the West Riding education authorities)

was to be, at the very best, undistinguished. In fact I learned very
little there except to drink, to be idle, and how to live, with some
help from like-minded companions, 'in a world of my own'. To be
an undergraduate at Oxford in the Thirties with very little money,
among those (though few at my college) who had a great deal, was
not necessarily a happy experience unless you had ambition of a
conventional kind or social graces, and I had not much of either.
So I have little to say of days of golden youth, of triumphs in Union
debates or at the OUDS, of afternoons spent with beautiful girls
in punts on the Cherwell, moored under the willow trees, of
conversations about the nature of reality protracted far into the
night in panelled rooms, of roaring off in sports cars to London, of
listening on May Morning to the choir singing on Magdalen Tower
– all those things which make up the sentimentally nostalgic idea
of being an undergraduate at Oxford in the Thirties.

My own experience – no doubt this was partly my own fault –
was not like that at all. But there were, of course, pleasant times
among the boring and the bad. I learned to enjoy a lot of music on
my portable, wind-up undergraduate's gramophone, and although
I did not read the books I was supposed to be reading and soon
stopped going to lectures, I read and absorbed for myself, in a
desultory way, more literature than I realised. As a youth, before
going to Oxford, I had read large parts of the *Encyclopaedia Britannica*
(11th edition) leaving out the articles on science and mathematics,
except those on astronomy, and in this way acquired an enormous
store of disorganised knowledge on all kinds of subjects from the
origin of the letter A to Zymotic Diseases (a term all the more
attractive for being described as obsolete).

During my second term at Oxford I got to know other undergraduates who were 'wasting their time' and taking no part in
university activities almost as determinedly as I was. Some of them
were the companions of my initiation into the pleasures of drinking,
and considering our generally meagre financial resources we got

through so much drink in that term that my staircase became known among the scouts, thanks to Sam, as 'the boozing staircase'.

As well as Alan Davis and myself, one of its occupants was David Thomson, who was to become a talented writer and, although we could not have foreseen this, an important figure in my life. He was then and remained afterwards a man of remarkable sweetness of character. He seemed entirely without self-consciousness. He was one of the few people I have known who were completely without pretence; unlike myself, who tended to be a different person with different people, he seemed not to take the slightest interest in who was who or how important or unimportant any particular person was or appeared to be; he was always himself.

This did not mean that he was free from nervousness. He often chewed up handkerchiefs without being aware of it. He was extremely short-sighted, but, physically as well as morally fearless, rode a bicycle though he could scarcely have seen beyond the handlebars, with an individual, zig-zag motion, a strange-looking figure in a thick white jersey and pebble glasses. He liked my jokes and fantastications. I was probably a bad influence on him; but for all his air of 'holy fool' he was no fool, though possibly holy.

Another friend or acquaintance at my college was a strange, flamboyant White Russian, Alexis Saburov, who wore bright blue silk shirts and affected homosexual leanings (then fashionable at Oxford) which I did not believe in. Even now, in spite of all I know to the contrary, I can hardly believe in the actual practice of sodomy and other perversions – I have always kept an element of West Riding commonsense, warring perpetually with other elements of my inheritance.

Saburov, who was much more a 'man of the world' than the rest of us, with more money and a background of mysterious grandeur, had a talent for getting systematically drunk in the Russian manner and organised our drinking in a most efficient way, making what might have been a mere barbarous enjoyment into a sophisticated entertainment. He was, of course, an extreme reactionary in politics as in everything else and introduced me to the dangerous writings of de Maistre and Houston Stewart Chamberlain, giving me a taste for geo-political speculation, one of the few proclivities I share with Adolf Hitler. He also confirmed and encouraged my own already reactionary views and consuming hatred of 'progress'.

He used to have 'self-pity hours' every Thursday afternoon at the Cadena Café in the 'Broad', with its wicker chairs, ladies' string trio and 'set teas' (the 'Lansdowne' or the 'Windsor' – 'pot of tea, bread and butter, scones, jam and slice of Genoa cake'). There he would sit for a whole hour by himself, the sentimental music in his ears, recalling in detail the humiliations and imperfections of his life until a satisfactory number of tears had run down his broad Russian cheeks; then, purged of all self-pity until next Thursday, he would rise, pay his bill with a lavish tip and bound into the bright, transfigured outer world, filled with self-confidence and satisfaction.

Saburov was a History Scholar, with an impressive library of his own which included many unusual, even exotic books. He was a dandy, wine-bibber and gourmet. Seized by a sudden desire for lobsters, he would buy a few, shut himself in his rooms ('sporting his oak') and consume them all by himself, with a bottle or two of champagne, emerging later with a catlike, satisfied if rather bloated look. Often drunk, he took pride in being able to sober up immediately if occasion – such as the sudden appearance of the Rector – required, becoming, in his own florid language, 'pale, grave, composed and noble' in an instant. To Sam he was a wonder and a mystery, 'a foreign young gentleman with a lot to say'. According to a story I heard much later, when we had both left Oxford, his end was premature and remarkable. Found in the gutter in Piccadilly, drunk or suffering from a fit brought on by over-eating, or both, he was carried into the Ritz

43

to die (a rare realisation of the catch-phrase 'he died as he would have wished').

Another friend and drinking companion at Lincoln at this time was Denis Hills, a big, handsome, fair-haired young man, a History Scholar from Birmingham, very charming and amusing, who was to have an eventful life in the Second World War and later as a wanderer about Africa, where he nearly met his end as a prisoner of Idi Amin, the tyrant of Uganda, saved at the last moment by James Callaghan, later Prime Minister.

It was about this time that Alan Davis's behaviour began to give the college authorities concern. Though senior, and reading for his Classical Finals, he was still, as a Scholar in his third year, living in college and on the boozing staircase. Always fond of drink, he was an occasional member of our circle, to which he contributed some of his store of mysterious knowledge. But anthroposophy does not go with alcohol, and it was alcohol which began to get the upper hand. Already, he claimed, he had been 'excommunicated' from the Salvation Army but *kept his trombone* (later on, as he sat playing it by the fire in some dismal bed-sitter in London, he related, an emissary of the Army who had tracked him down arrived to reclaim it, leaving a receipt).

He began to write and sing what later came to be called 'surrealist hymns' to Salvation Army tunes. I can still remember fragments of them. Here is one:

'I with my brand-new Belgian ophicleide,
Took it to church with me at Walrustide.
For the Holy Ghost is fond of toast,
And he brushes his hair with an old umbrella.'

Others were improvised from a single word or phrase, spoken or read in a newspaper, which his curious mind would seize upon:

'That he can;
In the Vatican
There are books of all sizes.
Some are the Pope's own Sunday School prizes.'

Or, more obscurely:

'What is a Stimfig?
A Stimfig is a man.
Billiards, he laiketh* billiards
For the North Ward Liberal clan.'

I remember one or two complete works:

'In the days of Fulke the Red,
The nuns all went to bed
With the mouth-organ hidden in the clothes;
And the Nonnë Priestess said
From the middle of the bed:
"Hark, hark, how soft the mistral blows".'

We spent quite a lot of time playing a game with very complicated rules: West Riding Knife Throwing. This involved throwing and catching by the handle, at high speed, a long, sharp kitchen knife. Our hands were often heavily bandaged. The college authorities seemed (though I don't suppose this was really so) to take no more notice of this than they did of any other features of what may be called an unremitting war on reality. There is no doubt that had we been undergraduates behaving in such a way fifty years later the authorities would have packed us all off to the psychiatrist; but as far as they were concerned psychiatry was then only just beginning to come in.

* 'Laike': West Riding dialect for 'play'.

45

However, Alan was sent out of college into lodgings. This did not improve matters. According to his own story his landlord took to persecuting him, writing anonymous letters to the college and following him about on a rusty old bicycle wherever he went. At last the college did take action, sending him off to the Littlemore Hospital to see Dr Neumann, a refugee from Germany who later, as a Flight Lieutenant in the Medical Branch of the RAF, had the task of attending every performance of Terence Rattigan's wartime play *Flight Path*, noting the reactions of the audience and producing statistical tables for analysis (I am not sure whether he got a medal for this, as he certainly deserved).

On a call for help from Alan, who feared he might be shut up in Littlemore by the sinister doctor, David Thomson and I set off to rescue him. We found him sitting in a nearby pub where, he said, he had taken refuge after distracting the doctor by telling him that smoke was coming out of his bookcase and then jumping out of the window. We thought the safest way to evade pursuit by the doctor and his white-coated assistants was to go to a small neighbouring railway station which was left mysteriously unmanned. We found a railway engine and actually contrived to make it travel over a short distance before we were spotted and ran for it.

But the college had had enough. Alan's scholarship was removed, which meant that he had to leave Oxford for good. It was a sorrowful business. At the time the college was installing a new organ in the chapel, and he composed a moving threnody to the tune of 'my bonnie lies over the ocean':

'My emoluments went into the organ,
My emoluments are under the key . . .
Bring back, bring back, oh bring back my
emoluments to me . . .'

So he left to make his fortune in London, wearing his black

46

Homburg ('Anthony Eden') hat, which we called the 'Hat of Peace', a pun on the Irish words 'sidh' and 'sioch' which anybody can work out for himself, and carrying a battered suitcase and a packet of cheese and tomato sandwiches as he walked away jerkily with one foot on the pavement and one in the gutter.

Meanwhile, in other realms, Hitler and the Nazis had risen to power. At that time I don't think I was greatly interested, regarding them at first as fabulous monsters and material for fantasy and later as unmistakable harbingers of war who provided another good reason for regarding Oxford, examinations, careers and 'all that sort of thing' as futile. None of my friends had any interest in politics except Denis Hills, who was at first attracted by the Nazi movement, though not for long, and Alexis Saburov, whose chief political aims, if he had any, were the restoration of the Tsar and the recovery of his own fabulous family estates in the Province of Orel.

We had a great contempt for the embryo politicians of the Oxford Union, in particular for one member of my college who talked of nothing but politics, hoped to become an MP (I dare say he did), and was once heard to boast: 'I left the debate just behind Michael Foot, and do you know, he let me help him on with his overcoat!'

I never asked myself what I would do when I left Oxford. It seemed inconceivable that we should ever leave it, or even that there was a world outside it. Whole days and weeks seemed to pass in idleness, in tiddleywink marathons or cricket-darts test match series, varied by occasional parties given by 'socially prominent' undergraduates where, sometimes as gatecrashers, we would pose unconvincingly as professional footballers or chemists' assistants.

Were there no girls in this curious, dreamlike existence? There were girls, but they belonged to a different order of things. From time to time I thought myself in love, sometimes extravagantly so, and even invited girls to my rooms during the permitted hours, up to 6 p.m., which were rigidly enforced by the porter, a saturnine man of splendid military bearing, whose eye nothing escaped. But I was shy and backward. I could not interpret the most obvious signals. I was also afraid of girls I thought beautiful and more at ease with those I did not, making the common mistake of the immature of supposing that attractive girls could not be intelligent or interesting to talk to.

As for going to bed with any girls, beautiful or otherwise, I doubt if I would have known what to do if I had ever got any to that point. Though considered very good-looking, I was or came to believe myself unattractive through rebuffs real or imaginary. Perhaps I was. I was ill-dressed and rather dirty, taking baths infrequently because I did not like the boisterous bathrooms of the college with their shouting and horseplay.

As for my studies, I took a poor Third in 'Honour Mods' in 1934, with an alpha in one paper only, on the satirist Juvenal. For 'Greats', my final examination, which I was due to take in 1936, I had to read philosophy and go to tutorials with the Rector himself, the bearded, precise and highly rational Dr Munro. We did not take to one another. I have a mind unapt for dealing with abstractions – perhaps unapt for sustained logical thought – and philosophy was not for me. After one term of hopeless floundering, I switched to what some called the 'soft option' of English (I have always had a passion for languages and Anglo-Saxon encouraged the interest I already had in the other, older languages of the British Isles). But I can't say I worked very hard at that either.

Although I went to very few lectures I did, of course, still have to visit my tutors from time to time to read essays to them aloud; I usually copied them almost verbatim from fairly obvious sources at the last possible moment, working far into the night. I could summon up enough impudence to read these wretched productions only after fortifying myself with two or three pints of strong ale. When the ordeal of reading was over, I scarcely listened to the long-suffering dons' comments before shambling from the room.

I had grown very far apart from my parents. But having no money or invitations elsewhere, or the hardihood to tramp the roads or join the Foreign Legion, I had to spend the greater part of my vacations with them. Their fortunes had now taken a curious turn. About the end of my second year at Oxford my father, although he could not have been much over fifty, decided to retire from the wool trade and, using most of what remained of his money, join my brother and his wife in a sheep farm bigger and better than Fell End, though even more remote.

It was in the wild upper reaches of the River Rawthey, on the border between Yorkshire and Westmorland, just within the former but with a postal address in the latter – 'near Ravenstonedale' (how proudly I had this romantic address engraved, in Saburovian splendour, on my visiting cards!). It was on the western side of Wild Boar Fell, a place to suit my brother's obsessive love of distancing himself from all the human race except his admirable wife, and, as far as I was concerned, a place where I could wander in solitude as I pleased, in glorious contrast to my life at Oxford.

There my father and mother, attended by 'Aunt', who after a brief escape into employment with the wife of the Vicar of Shipley, who thought her ill-treated, had been summoned back to serfdom, moved with the remnants of their impedimenta – the Chippendale chairs, the mahogany sideboard with its silver candlesticks, the Dresden figurines, the bridge tables, the art nouveau chromium standardlamps, the dining table with its thick slab of plate glass. Never can a rough Westmorland farmhouse have been so incongruously furnished. And never can there have been an arrangement, even among my family's arrangements, so obviously doomed to failure.

It was not long before my father got Bell's Palsy, an ailment

49

usually associated with worry, which caused the left side of his face to drop and gave him a strange appearance which aroused shouts of laughter whenever he appeared. He seemed an old man already, partly because he liked, for his own masochistic reasons, to pose as old, and partly because he was continually told so. The only duty about the farm he was thought capable of was feeding the hens which clucked about in their small field beyond the muddy, cow-mucky back yard and the outdoor privy. A scene comes to my mind's eye from that time: my father, tottering along (or 'crammling' as 'Aunt' called it in her personal dialect) towards the front door of the house with his empty hen-food bucket, entering and putting it down on the mahogany sideboard between the silver candlesticks, with a look half rueful and half satisfied at his absurd abasement.

This set off a row in the old style as my mother began upbraiding him for 'spoiling her nice things'. There were a lot of rows, and although my brother did not like them he was at least used to them, and may have thought them a price worth paying for the possession of the farm. His wife, unused to the exotic goings-on of exotic people, was upset by them; and even more upset by my mother's attitude to her, which became, as memories of past grandeur grew ever grander, the attitude of a fine lady to a humble farmer's daughter. The resulting troubles were always blamed on my father. At the time I accepted this. But, as I later realised with remorse, that ineffectual and kindly man was hardly at all to blame. Nor was my poor, deluded mother. It was all an 'inherent contradiction'.

My brother, for all the element of desperate play-acting in his role of sheep farmer, was, I think, a very competent one. He certainly worked hard enough for two; he even contrived to put twice as much energy into whistling at his sheep dogs as any indigenous farmer would have done. At haytime he turned into a positive tyrant in his determination to get his one big field of hay into his barns – rising at dawn to beat the weather and using the uncertain headlights of his ancient Riley car to supplement moonlight. The hay was mown by a horse-drawn mower. Then it was spread in long rows across the field and had to be dried by a laborious process of raking over by hand. The poor old horse was managed by Old Jack, our 'hind', or labourer, a solitary man who looked as if he were made out of the rocks of his native Westmorland. He seldom spoke, but incessantly chewed tobacco, regarding it as unworthy of a man, indeed almost effeminate, to smoke it. He refused my father's offer of a Havana with scorn. My father bravely accepted his offer of a plug, but turned green after a few minutes' chewing.

'I'll have no passengers on this farm!' shouted my brother in his ever more convincing Westmorland voice, as he urged on his labour force whenever the weather was suitable for turning the hay, and sometimes when it wasn't – a gleam of sunshine between showers was enough to produce a frenzy of activity. So my mother, my father, 'Aunt' and myself toiled away with our rakes in the sun, helped by one of those Irishmen, all called 'Paddy', who came, often from the poorest and most remote parts of the West, to supplement the haytime workers on all but the poorest farms. Our wild Westmorland must have seemed a tame and highly civilised place to these temporary migrants from their land of rocks, potato patches and straggling fuchsia hedges. To my brother's fury, our own 'Paddy' was delighted when it rained. He could spend his time sleeping in a barn or playing ha'penny Nap with Old Jack, and still get his few pounds' wages at the end.

When the hay was dry it was heaped up in haycocks (I enjoyed constructing these) and then came the last frenzied operation – loading it on a cart and leading the horse to the barns where we, the menfolk, that is, forked it in with pitchforks, my brother making the final adjustments within. My father's ineptitude with the pitchfork was remarkable and the cause of endless mockery. Once, when he was wielding his fork and smoking one of his last Havanas – a decidedly foolhardy thing to do, since it might have sent the precious hay up in flames and, though this might have been thought of less account, burned him to death – my brother angrily snatched away both fork and cigar. He kept the cigar butt for making one or more of the hand-rolled cigarettes he kept in a secret, personal store.

It was, of course, traditional to provide 'drinkings' for the toilers in the hayfield – the Irishmen would not have worked without it – during their brief periods of necessary rest. The 'drinkings' my brother provided were not lavish – a few stone jars of cider, which my father supplemented with some bottles of Grand Marnier, Cointreau and other liqueurs he had salvaged from his Harrogate cellars. It was pleasant, on a hot summer's day, to sit drinking in the long grass in a shady corner of the field. With my superior Oxford expertise I drank more than anybody else, sometimes lingering overlong while the rest were at their ancient, backbreaking task, and even daring to defy my brother's angry eye before joining them with infuriating languor. Because I lived there only part of the time I was a liberated serf.

One very hot day, when we were working in the field, 'Aunt', who had been sent to the house to get some bread and cheese – because of her notorious rock-hard buns and coagulated puddings she was not trusted with anything else – suddenly rushed out and shouted the single word 'Joescum!' What had happened was that my mother's bother Joe, who lived in Manchester and was something of a ne'er-do-well, the black sheep of the Wharton family, had taken it into his head to pay us a visit, walking ten miles from the nearest station, Kirkby Stephen. He was said to 'like a drink' – a sure sign of depravity in my mother's family. He was parched. But with scarcely a word said he had a rake thrust into his hand and was propelled into the field to join the line of rakers. 'It's like t'Khyber Pass here,' he said, looking round at the wild surroundings in amazement and adjusting a knotted handkerchief on his already reddening bald head. Henceforth – and, bearing no ill-will, he made several uninvited appearances – he was always known as 'Joescum'. This became another of those arcane terms particularly relished by my father, which had only to be pronounced, à propos of nothing, to have everybody falling about with amusement. Even my brother would take a moment off to smile.

But hard as he worked and hard as he strove to be like them, the neighbouring farmers – there were three or four other farms scattered within two or three miles – did not like him. What could people called Fothergill or Metcalfe, whose forebears had lived in this rough place for hundreds of years, make of a newcomer called Nathan, who arrived out of nowhere with a strange, incongruous entourage?

What could they make of my father, with his habit of rolling on the floor in simulated agony and his fondness for expensive chocolates and marrons glacés, which still arrived occasionally from a shop in Harrogate or even, for all I know, from Fortnum and Mason? What could they make of 'Aunt', who in her meagre spare time still searched the pastures for comfrey and sometimes, out of habit, tried to accompany me on my wanderings on the fells? What could they make of me? 'Thoo's a big lad to be still at school,' said Old Jack.

The landlord of my brother's farm and a few others was Dr Frankland, who lived at Needlehouse, a picturesque place, quite large but of no great age, down in the hollow by the rushing river, surrounded by gloomy pine trees. He was a learned man and a romantic, and his romance was Norway and the Norsemen who had colonised this neighbourhood, perhaps by way of Ireland, a thousand years before. He rode a fine black fell pony, with a big knife in an ornate scabbard of Norse design at his side. His children, then quite young, have made some mark in the world since; he had named them Raven, Noble and Helga, names resonant of the hard, bitter north which belonged to the people he loved, the colonisers of Iceland and Vinland.

What the Franklands made of our ménage I cannot say. One day Mrs Frankland invited us all to tea – except for my brother, who was too busy for inessential things. It was a strange occasion. We sat in her pleasant middle-class sitting-room, with its 'good' furniture, which looked out on the small lawn, with a few flower-beds, in the narrow space between the house and the river foaming among rocks – my father, my mother, my brother's wife, 'Aunt' and myself. Although Mrs Frankland must have known I was at Oxford she did not mention this, perhaps regarding it as something too absurdly incongruous to accept. I did not speak but rudely fell, as I often did, into a sort of waking dream, in which the sound of the river merged with the murmur of voices. My father, who was wearing one of his old Savile Row suits, did not speak much either.

My brother's wife – apart from Mrs Frankland perhaps the only sensible person present – talked of the affairs of the farm and of the small flower-garden she was trying to create in a corner of the garth. But her remarks and Mrs Frankland's were gradually overborne by a dialogue between my mother and 'Aunt'. My poor mother was doing her best and producing, in her efforts to assert herself, some remarkable phonemes. But by some mischance 'Aunt' had begun to talk about the mysterious symptoms her sister, 'Black Draught Annie', had developed lately – red spots which appeared on her forehead whenever she drank tea. 'It was on a Wednesday.' 'Aunt' recommended comfrey. My mother brushed this suggestion aside, recalling Dr Nimmo-Watson's panacea, lemon juice. 'Besides,' she said, 'they want to get rid of that dog, Spot – I'm sure it's unhealthy – only Herbert won't hear of it. It wants putting down at that age,' she said, appealing to Mrs Frankland's commonsense. 'Aunt' began muttering about a neighbour of Mrs Hall, the Shipley vicar's wife, who had suffered from *blue* spots after drinking tea.

Although there had been no mention of 'Black Draught Annie's' digestive troubles, my father suddenly exploded in helpless laughter. My mother rose to her feet in indignation and alarm. Anything could have happened. But at that moment Bodo, the now aged Aberdeen which was one of our remaining links with 'Duchy Grange', rushed past the window in one of his hysterical fits, pursued by a sheep dog. The party broke up and as far as I know there was no second invitation.

Our strange ménage was now under many tensions. My brother's wife was quite often in tears, her flower-garden belittled ('Lund!' my father would say to offset my mother's references to her Harrogate parterres, but even this magic formula for relief by laughter failed to work, for lack of a quorum which it could act on), her supposedly lowly origins in Swaledale contrasted with her husband's expensive education in Switzerland. Threatened with a miscarriage, she had to go to the nearest suitable hospital, in Preston. We all piled into my brother's car, which smelled strongly of the sheep he often carried in it, and he drove us erratically southwards (his driving was like everything else about him, energetic to the point of frenzy, involving much agonised grinding of gears). On our return the engine boiled on a steep hill and when we were nearing home on the rough farm track one of the back wheels came off, rolling in front of the car in a way which surprised us all. Finding that the car remained stable, my brother, I think, might not have troubled to put the wheel on again if my father had not insisted, maddened by bleating noises from the back of the car, coming either from a sheep which had got into the party without being noticed or, more likely, from 'Aunt'.

The ménage was becoming intolerable. There was trouble with a neighbouring farmer who, finding some of my brother's sheep intruding on his land, cut off their toes. There was a court case. My brother was awarded damages, but this did not help him in the eyes of the indigenous farmers who may, for all I knew, have thought this primitive brutality quite excusable, even laudable. Did Dr Frankland, dreaming of Viking days, wonder whether there were grounds for a blood-feud, a fight to the death with axes, while overhead the eagles screamed? My own cruel fantasies certainly ran on those lines.

Many years later I found among my 'papers' a photograph, already turning brown, which seemed to sum up our life at that time. It showed (I no longer have it; it has mysteriously disappeared) a group of us lined up in front of the door of the farmhouse on a gloomy October day. There was my father, a short, paunchy figure with a kindly lop-sided smile, clutching his hen-food bucket; my mother, also short, dressed in town clothes, wearing a pearl necklace and a large emerald ring; my brother, his lean brown face full of impatience at this waste of time, dressed in farmer's gear and carrying a shepherd's crook, topped with a ram's horn, which for all I know he had made himself; his wife, smiling a pleasant smile and standing out among the rest by her wholesome, natural appearance; 'Joescum', evidently on one of his periodical visits, looking as if he could do with a drink; 'Aunt' staring madly at the camera with folded arms, wearing what looked like a flattened fireman's hat; and myself, sinister in an idiotic way, with long, untidy hair and stubbly cheeks, holding a large, late mushroom. We looked like a group of partisans – hopelessly inefficient ones – rounded up by the Germans in the Second World War somewhere in the forests of Volhynia and about to be herded off and shot. Who took this photograph? Perhaps it was a passing sheep.

It cannot have been long after this that my father decided to cut his losses (among other things he had had a bath installed at great expense, though there was still no indoor lavatory) and moved with my mother back to Bradford, where he took up a rather humble job in some old friend's wool firm. Apart from the absurdity of this attempt to live an impossible life with a daughter-in-law my mother could not get on with, that was a bad time for farming. His losses must have been considerable. But he was able to afford a pleasant enough flat in Manningham, near Lister Park and not far from 'Oakleigh', symbol, to him sad and majestic, of a life which had gone for ever.

Back at Oxford my life of mingled torpor, drunkenness and general oddity had lost some of its flavour with the departure of Alan Davis. He now lived in London, supporting himself or being supported as best he could. At one time he lodged in a tiny, totally unfurnished room in a flat in one of the less socially acceptable mansion blocks in Prince of Wales Drive in Battersea, one of those London streets which 'everybody' is said to live in at one time or another (and where, many years later, I was to live myself). His landlord, typically enough, was a religious maniac, a former contemporary of his at Lincoln who had left after trying to commit suicide in his rooms in an unusually elaborate way. He rigged up a hammock between a bookcase and the cupboard where he kept his fruitcake and supply of mineral-water, drank half a bottle of whisky, swallowed some aspirins, climbed into the hammock and set fire to it. He had overlooked the matter of smoke, which at once alerted the porter, who removed the babbling man calmly and efficiently, with a piece of advice: 'Take my word for it, sir, a carving knife is the best thing. But do try to make as little mess as possible. It's not fair on the scouts.'

The 'boozing staircase' was not so agreeable as it had been. One evening, a group of public school freshmen, annoyed by our unacceptable attempt to combine boozing with poetry, the fascist philosophy of Alexis Saburov and the incessant playing of Mozart's chamber music on my gramophone – they believed, perhaps rightly, that undergraduates should be 'hearties' or 'aesthetes' but not both – attacked my rooms. Their idea was to put Saburov, a foreigner, reputed homosexual and therefore the most objectionable member of the gang, under the pump in the front quad – a traditional punishment. I produced an antique horse-pistol which some girl had given me as a token of esteem and, pointing it at the leader of the lynch party, put them to flight (they returned later on, of course, and gave Saburov, who screamed in an unseemly foreign manner like a stuck pig, a thorough sousing).

Summoned before the Dean next day to account for my horse-pistol – the use of firearms in college, particularly for such a purpose, was a serious offence – I pulled the weapon from under my coat. 'Don't point that thing at me!' he shouted. 'It might go off!' I showed him that it was impossible to fire it. After warning me against such breaches of discipline, he let me go. But it was another black mark to add to my dossier of offences – some comparatively conventional, such as letting off fire-extinguishers – others less so, such as carrying about a large brass doorknob and letting it fall to the ground with a mysterious clang during lectures or even tutorials, then disclaiming all responsibility.

I was moving away from my boon companions (or, more likely, they from me) and becoming more and more of a solitary creature. Sometimes, in the evenings, I used to wander into the part of Oxford called St Ebbe's (it has since been flattened to make car parks, council flats, 'precincts' and supermarkets), a mysterious place, the dankest, most permanently autumnal quarter of that dank, autumnal city. I had discovered, somewhere in that maze of undistinguished streets, a small, shabby, wholly undistinguished pub. Here, in a brown parlour with a cracked, out-of-tune piano and dusty photographs of long-dead jockeys on the walls, I played a simple variant of dominoes for half pints of beer with undersized, secretive men who sometimes changed the rules, such as they were, in mid-game.

Some of them, men with flat, opaque eyes in sallow faces, descended perhaps from the marsh-dwellers of Otmoor, may have been related to college servants, judging from the bags of assorted food – mostly curling anchovy toast or, in summer, lobster mayonnaise and strawberries – they often had with them. Their conversation was about missing bicycles, varieties of soap or the best ways of catching rats.

It was hard to say if these strange people accepted me. Sometimes, bemused by beer and dominoes, I passed into a trancelike state in which they seemed not so much human beings as a crowd of rain-worn sundials and clock-faces, whose sighing breath lifted the frayed linoleum at my feet with a soothing, rhythmic motion. They did not seem to mind.

One summer vacation, after I had come into a tiny legacy, I spent almost all of it on a solitary three weeks' walking-tour in the West of Ireland. Horribly sea-sick on the night boat from Liverpool to Dublin through drinking Guinness all night with a crowd of people who looked at me with suspicion because of my Oxford 'aesthete's' purple shirt and green velvet tie but were willing enough to accept rounds of drinks, I staggered into bed at Jury's hotel, then spent a few days wandering about Dublin before catching a train to Sligo, sacred birthplace of my hero Yeats.

From there I walked by stages through Mayo to Galway, thence by train to Dublin and so back to England. I can remember every detail of this trip – the hotels, dirty and primitive, with little but 'fry ups' to offer by way of food; the fine, wild country, with its daily stint of rain and multiple rainbows; the mountains – one, Nephin in Mayo, made a peculiar impression on me, though I was riddled with flea-bites from the hotel on the shore of Loch Conn – the places by the wayside where I rested with my stick and knapsack among the rocks.

Did I enjoy all this? It is hard to say. I hardly spoke to a soul except in the way of asking directions or blunderingly seeking a bed for the night. It was a kind of escape, but I cannot say what I was escaping from unless it were myself. There was a certain self-consciousness in my progress through these regions, so long imagined from my addiction to the illusory 'Celtic' world. I took a bus from Galway to Gort and stood in ritual homage by Yeats's Tower, with its stone bridge over the gliding stream, then, after a statutory time, walked back. The poet was not there (it did not look as if anybody at all had ever lived there). If he had come out and spoken to me I doubt if I could have thought of anything to say.

On the day I took the boat back to England, I had a solitary luncheon at Jammet's, then the most famous restaurant in Dublin, perhaps the only one worthy of the name. In a ritual, self-conscious manner, I ordered an absurd, Saburovian and very expensive meal, accompanied, I think, by the *wrong kind of wine*, and finishing with a large Havana cigar. Without knowing it, I was falling into the very same state of incongruity which annoyed and embarrassed me so much in the case of my own family. Back at Oxford, Saburov was abandoning his humbler friends, myself included, for what he called, with an outrageous flourish, 'birds of finer feather', the cosmopolitan people of the continual parties, the 'celebrities' who figured in *Isis*, the Oxford magazine. Unequipped either with money or social ease, I tried to emulate him. It is a time I cannot recall without shame – the rebuffs, the awkward silences, the absurd snobberies which I tolerated, even tried to share in, the foolish pursuit of smart, sophisticated girls who, if they noticed me at all, looked through me, the rejection of pleasant, unsmart girls who were no doubt just as good to look at and much more agreeable to talk to than those female chimeras.

A perceptive young French Jew at my college called Reinach, member of a distinguished family, said to me after we had both been at one of these parties so coveted by me, but to him, no doubt, a matter of course: 'You are a strange person, Michael. I cannot understand how anyone can be at the same time so civilised and intelligent and yet so stupid and boorish.' It would certainly have been hard to explain this to him, even if I had understood it myself.

Would a visit to Bradford or Westmorland – supposing such a thing were conceivable – have enlightened this well-mannered, handsome young man who was often to be seen that summer lying in the cushions of a punt on the Cherwell, while some adoring young woman of the sort I lusted after so vainly poled him gracefully along? A dark thought sounds like a harsh-toned bell through this trivial chronicle – what became of young Reinach when, six years later, the Germans conquered France?

At the end of my second year I moved out of college into lodgings. I chose some rooms in Holywell Street, just opposite what were then the Oxford University Music Rooms. They were pleasant rooms on the first floor, much better than my rooms in college and, in accord with my general defiance of reality and attempts to emulate Saburov, more expensive than I could afford. The landlady, Mrs Gems, a widow who lived in her own mysterious quarters below with her elder sister, was heard to say I was a very quiet, pleasant young gentleman. Before long, like Sam, she had cause to revise her opinion.

Partly to get away from Bradford and partly with the idea of turning over a new leaf and actually doing some work for my Finals, I arrived a week or so before term started. On a fine, sunny October morning I sat down to the first of Mrs Gems's breakfasts, rather more content with myself than usual, and read in the morning paper which she had brought – it was *The Times*, my reaction to my parents' invariable *Daily Mail* – that King Alexander of Yugoslavia and the French Foreign Minister had been assassinated at Marseilles. This meant little to me. I had no great interest in politics, though next year I was to be indignant at Mussolini's invasion of Abyssinia, perhaps the first and only time I have ever felt any twinges of liberal feeling. Was it because Abyssinia and its Emperor, the Lion of Judah, the strange, savage mountain monasteries of the Coptic-descended church, the Amharic language and its peculiar alphabet, the exotic rituals of a barbaric court had somehow become a cherished bit of the knowledge-hoard accumulated through all that reading of the *Encyclopaedia Britannica*?

My resolve to work did not last long. Soon I was drinking as much as ever. My sitting-room overlooked the street and had a pleasant window seat, a strong temptation to sit doing nothing except stare out of the window at passers-by, turning them into the creatures of comic fantasy I liked so much. I was already convinced that I would become a 'great writer', both poet and novelist. A habit of turning real people, even people I liked, into fictional characters was, of course, deeply rooted in me from childhood on – it was one of the things that separated me from people, and made me a sort of emotional cripple. It was defensive and essentially feeble, but to many people it made me seem arrogant, haughty and even, absurdly enough, mature beyond my years. My friend David Thomson wrote at this time in some notes for a novel I took a look at one day when he was out of his rooms: 'He seemed to look at people as though they were animals at a fair.' This was true and perceptive. But did he realise what lay behind this unpleasing attitude?

Soon I was at my old tricks again, playing my personal game of social snakes and ladders in which there were only a few short ladders and many long snakes. I drank a lot, sometimes with my old college friends, who were all in lodgings themselves in different parts of Oxford; sometimes alone. Towards the end of that term I was 'gated' for the rest of it – confined to my lodgings after nine o'clock at night. I cannot even remember what offence I had committed – perhaps it was persistent drinking in pubs, which undergraduates were then forbidden to visit by the university rules. I had become friendly with a girl who was studying at the Ruskin School of Art and lived with a woman friend in a curious shanty, liable to flooding, by the Cherwell. On the last night of the term I 'broke my gating' by climbing out of my lodgings – it was quite easy, a simple jump from the broad lintel over the front door – to spend the night with her.

It was the first time I had been to bed with a girl. In a technical sense it was a chaste occasion.

Next day I found that Mrs Gems, who had been eyeing me more and more malevolently, and with good reason – she had amended her original impression of me to 'a quiet gentleman but he has such noisy friends' – had informed the Dean of my college that I was absent. It was the day of 'Responsions', a short, intermediate written examination taken in the college hall. I turned up looking tousled and wearing – a silly badge of bravado – a girl's 'kirby grip' stuck in my hair. Soon I was summoned to see the Rector. His manner was cold, his words few. 'You have a good brain but you refuse to use it. You are rusticated for the whole of next term. You will leave Oxford immediately. I cannot say what attitude the – er – ' he consulted some notes with distaste, his pointed beard quivering slightly – 'I cannot say what attitude the West Riding Education Committee will take in the matter of continuing your scholarship.' He obviously hoped they would discontinue it. I left, and as I crossed his small rectorial garden, deliberately walked on the dewy grass and left my evil trail on it. Though slightly stunned, I laughed. Wasn't this what always happened to great, romantic writers in their youth?

Unwilling to go back to Bradford to face my parents with my disgrace – I had long assumed that although my mother would not hear a word against me, neither of them would understand anything I did or why I did it, and therefore never told them anything – I did not leave Oxford immediately either. I stole a few books and sold them – another romantic gesture of genius. With my girl I spent several days and nights living in the rooms, mainly in New College, I think, of undergraduates who had gone down for the vacation, occasionally entertaining such friends as David Thomson and Denis Hills. It is amazing that we were not detected. There was a popular tune of that time, 'Lost in a Fog' – other favourites which come to mind now with unearthly, nostalgic force are 'Stormy Weather' and 'The Last Round Up' – which expressed our mood completely. I was lost in a fog, not so much of love – though there was love, certainly on her part – as of romantic illusion.

We travelled north and spent several weeks in a tumbledown cottage in Yorkshire which some kind friend had lent us. We had little enough to eat, but the howling gales and rainstorms suited our mood. Sometimes there were wonderful days of winter sunshine and diamond frost, with icicles inside the small panes of the cottage windows. We would walk for miles in the lonely countryside, eating and drinking supplies of expensive food and wine in the Saburovian tradition which I ordered on the various accounts I had at shops in Oxford. Boxes of Havana cigars and of the then fashionable black Russian cigarettes were delivered. We had my portable undergraduate's gramophone, but all my records had been lost or stolen during our adventures – except one, Brahms's String Quartet in C Minor, with its sad, hesitant slow movement which my girl said was like a bird with a broken wing. She often said such things and I did not count them against her.

One day I was summoned to Wakefield, the headquarters of the West Riding County Council, to explain myself to members of the education committee. The Rector of Lincoln's hopes were not realised. The committee were surprisingly sympathetic, obviously puzzled by a paradox: that I, who looked so bookish and seemed so quiet, should go in for such harum-scarum doings as spraying fire-extinguishers and climbing at night over college roofs. They evidently thought I looked – as I probably did – like the sort of undergraduate, with a Jewish name into the bargain – who would get fire-extinguishers sprayed over *him*. They forgave me, exhorted me to do better and be myself in future. I said I would try. But how could I be myself? It was the very last thing I wanted to be.

Next term – the summer term – was windy and sad at Oxford. By courtesy of Mrs Gems, I was back in my old lodgings. I made one or two new friends who, though they did not belong to Saburov's 'lofty circle', as he called it, were sometimes mentioned in *Isis*. I also genuinely liked them. Saburov once said, in his flamboyant way, when, having drunk too much, I was about to vomit with as much neatness as I could manage into a large magenta-coloured vase, 'the cold white serpent coiled about his heart has risen to his cheeks'. Whatever he and others might say, I was not incapable of human feelings.

One of my new friends was the kind, clever and attractive Sally Graves, niece of Robert Graves. Another, also at Somerville, was Eithne Wilkins, a big, blonde girl with a delightful, deep, affected voice, who, crippled in one hip by polio, walked with a strange, swaying motion. She was well thought of as a poet at Oxford in those days, writing under the name of Eithne nic Liamóig – 'Eithne the Daughter of Little William', an ingenious Gaelicised version of her name. Her poems were eloquent and extremely obscure, making my own seem simple-minded and derivative. She found my fantasticated jokes amusing, and thus encouraged by somebody I could both like and respect, I became good company for her, though instantly lapsing into painful silence when her 'important' friends were present.

Eithne was, I suppose, in love with me. But she did not mind that I was only a friend in return. Years later, at the end of the war, she was to marry a German-Jewish refugee, Ernst Kaiser, like herself a genuine intellectual, no pseudo-intellectual like myself. Together they translated the works of the unreadable Robert Musil and became the greatest authorities in the world on his life and work. Such was to be Eithne's niche in literature, and not the poet's fame I supposed would certainly be hers.

What did we talk about, what did we do in those concluding days of my time at Oxford? I can hardly remember. At the beginning of my final year I moved from Holywell to new, humbler lodgings in Wellington Square. I had a sitting-room on the ground floor from which I could see across the square the room of an undergraduate unknown to me – he was one of those who wore yellow shirts with blue ties and vice versa, one of those I thought most enviable – who constantly entertained girls of the kind I always wanted and never got. How often, as I sat at my desk, reading *Beowulf* or Spenser, or trying to read them, did I watch in jealous anguish the arrival of these girls, whether small and boyish or tall and elegant! Why did they seem so infinitely more desirable than any girls I knew myself? Perhaps they were. But, as I recall those futile afternoons and feel again the rigidity which was the physical expression of a locked and paralysed will, I think the fault was in myself and in my own perverted eyes.

I did not spend all my time in such futile ways. I read a great deal, learning to enjoy – it was almost the keenest enjoyment I knew – English poetry which was not on my set books – Hopkins, Pound, Eliot. And, sometimes alone, sometimes with friends, I made excursions on foot or bicycle into the haunted countryside round Oxford, to Otmoor or Wychwood Forest, one of the ancient royal hunting forests of England whose largest remnant, still magical and mysterious, is within the big park of Cornbury House, the one house in all England which I most covet and would choose should a grateful nation ever ask me what reward I wanted for my services. There were many times, amid the boredom and jealousy, when the old sense of the numinous, springing from some combination of light and colour, or contour of fields, woods and hills, assured me that all was not lost.

At the end of that last Hilary term of 1936, I quarrelled with my girl – I had met some other girl I found attractive and who showed signs of not rebuffing me – and went off to Bradford to stay in my parents' flat and make a last desperate effort to catch up on my work so as to get a degree of some sort, however lowly. I felt relieved at the break, then guilty. So when my girl rang up one day and asked if we could make it up and could she come to Bradford, I did not demur. My mother, ever indulgent and liking the girl, did not demur either. My father, who was sinking into an apathy which only furtive betting and the company of low companions could relieve, made no complaint.

There was nothing much to do in Bradford and I could not settle to my books. It was late March; the trees in the park were leafless; their smoke-blackened boughs were set against a dead-white sky; gardeners were busy among the still wintry paths and beds; we read; my girl did some sketching and painting; we walked about the peculiar half-country on the edge of Bradford, looking towards the moors. Suddenly I began writing a 'novel', typing a few pages as I had so often done before on my big, solid portable before giving up. This time I did not give up.

What I was producing was a nightmarish vision of a city in the West Riding, based on Bradford, of course, whose civic leaders suddenly decide to declare its independence. The central character, a retired army officer who has formerly travelled in Tibet, is visiting the city to give a lecture on that country and is caught up in the collective fantasy of the independence movement; he tries to leave but finds it more and more difficult until at last he is completely trapped. The book, in fact, has a moral lesson against getting involved in fantasies which are really of your own making. In a way it described my own condition. But I did not think of it in that way when I was writing it. I tried to mingle Gothic beauty with grotesque humour.

Once I had got beyond the first chapter, I worked on, day after day. Never in my life, I think, before or since, have I been so completely absorbed in any task as I was in writing this book. It took me about six months of concentrated work. Back at Oxford my Finals, which came when I had written about three-quarters of the book, seemed merely a nuisance and intrusion. I did not even bother, when sitting the examination, to answer the questions but answered others which I made up to pass the time.

In fact I was only allowed to take the examination at all by what I now see was the extreme good nature of the authorities. I had been technically sent down just beforehand, partly for the mass-destruction of crockery and throwing a Scotch egg at the high table in hall, and partly for an unusual offence which compounded those rather commonplace ones: dismantling a huge old Victorian sofa in order to throw it out of the window of an empty room in my college. I spent a whole day on this task, while various undergraduates looked in from time to time to see how I was getting on or ask if they could lend a hand. This I declined.

The defenestration of the sofa, like the writing of my book, I saw as my task alone. I had got the back and legs off and had the main bulk of the thing half out of the window when the authorities intervened, indicting me for what was, though not so described at the time, the culmination of a whole series of unprovoked attacks upon furniture. The incident has found its way into fiction and memoirs, sometimes attributed to others. But whether it is a matter for pride or shame, or both, or neither, I claim it as my own.

When the farce of the examination was over, I took leave of Oxford under the statutory cloud (seen off at the station by my only remaining friend at Lincoln, David Thomson, with his habitual air of rueful, puzzled concern and goodwill), and went to Bournemouth, where my girl had taken a job as a waitress. I hired a bed-sitter in some tree-lined road, finished my book, typed out three copies of all 120,000 words of it, sent one to a London literary agent I had met on my journey in Ireland, then got married to my girl at the local registry office with two taxi drivers for witnesses. We returned to Oxford, where I was due to take my 'Viva', immediately after-wards.

In the train I glanced at the stop-press in a newspaper. It mentioned, among the racing results and cricket scores, that a

Spanish general, Francisco Franco, had started a revolt against the Socialist government. When I took the 'Viva' next morning, quite early, I realised that I had over-prepared myself for this nerve-wracking event. I must have been one of the most drunken under-graduates ever to appear before the examiners. Next day we bought bicycles and set off from Oxford, I for the last time *in statu pupillari*, in a north-westerly direction.

That we should make for Wales was natural enough, for I had long been interested in it. I had read Borrow's *Wild Wales* too (he has always had a subversive, unsettling influence), but there was a good deal of difference between the middle-aged Borrow who tramped through Wales with his big green umbrella in the 1850s, asking all he met what various monticles and precipices were called, showing off his Welsh and searching out the graves of famous Welsh poets, and the young man and woman who wandered about the beautiful wild recesses of Wales in the summer of 1936.

We soon ditched our bicycles, perhaps because of mechanical defects, and took to walking. I cannot remember what my wife wore. But I myself, in order to cope with all kinds of weather, wore a thick black overcoat and a black 'hat of peace'. For luggage we both carried stout shopping bags with a few pairs of socks and other odd articles of clothing. We were determined, I suppose, not to be taken for hikers or to be conventional in any way. Heaven knows what romantic nonsense we talked as we crossed the Cotswolds as quickly as possible, then made for Ross-on-Wye and our first objective, the Black Mountains, whose name had long intrigued me.

We stayed in the Abbey hotel at Llanthony, where Landor once had lived, then crossed over the Bwlch yr Efengyl by what was then a rough, stony track (it is now a traffic jam at week-ends) into the Wye Valley. We laughed, we sang, we quarrelled sometimes, made up, grew browner every day as we crossed the great 'Welsh Desert', then a wonderful empty expanse, a place of freedom, with not a single sitka spruce tree in sight. Those green and golden hillsides were alive with larks and grazed by innumerable sheep. We reached the sea at Aberystwyth, then turning back with an instinct for solitude which, though I did not realise it, was not unlike my brother's, crossed over the hills again.

One night we slept in the haunted park of Hafod, huddled together for warmth and waking to find my hat full of snails, the next in some wayside pub under the shoulder of Plynlimon, then turned north-west again towards Machynlleth and the sea, then zig-zagged back to Bala. We stayed that night at the best hotel in that intensely Welsh town, then turned resolutely west towards the higher mountains.

We meant to spend that night in a barn in sight of Arenig Fawr, a wild, unvisited mountain which seemed and still seems (and not for me only) to have a special, magical essence more powerful than the more famous mountains of Wales. Escaping from a fierce stallion in a field by sacrificing our last scrap of food, a banana, we stumbled across the cottage where, unknown to us, Augustus John had stayed before the First World War, and met with true Welsh hospitality – a feather-bed, a good breakfast and no questions asked of this odd pair as we set off again next morning through the solitudes of Migneint towards the mountains of Gwynedd.

What use is a catalogue of places? I remember now our innocence and health, our immersion in the world of the senses in jewel-bright Wales. We met various odd characters, genuine tramps, people (mostly English) who wondered what we were at and, once, a stern Welsh minister who gave us a lecture, not on morals (though I doubt he believed the evidence of my young wife's wedding ring) but on the glories of the Welsh nation and on the foolish Saxons who held it of such small account. I listened, not telling him that he was preaching to the converted. I was silent and withdrawn with strangers, dependent on my wife's easy chatter. Sometimes she would tell me I should smile a bit more. I tried it once or twice, but soon forgot – a joke which fortunately we could share.

Sometimes I would fall into sadness, and knew that she neither shared nor understood it. Could this sadness, which came and went without apparent reason, have been brought on not only by my innate melancholy but by ghosts from the future, ghosts of myself, who was to visit these places so often long afterwards, in different circumstances, when the rough tracks had turned to metalled motor-roads and the green paths were classified and waymarked, no tramp or pseudo-tramp, but in comfort, with money in my pocket, but without her?

This aimless wandering might have gone on for ever, or at least until winter came. But a time came when we turned, without quite knowing why, back towards England. We settled down in a fusty old furnished cottage with a fine big orchard we found on the Herefordshire border. There on an evil day, with autumn coming on, the typescript of my book came thudding through the door – rejected, even by the literary agent! This was a terrible blow. In my arrogant simplicity I had never even thought of such a possibility. I fell into one of my fits of miserable torpor, a particularly bad one this, and even took to my bed. Always able to produce symptoms of illness at will, I ran quite a high fever. My wife, alarmed, sent for the doctor from the nearby market town.

Dr Kingdom, a portly, middle-aged man with a black bag, eyed me, took my temperature, hummed faintly to himself, then stood for a long time staring out of the window at the copious apples hanging all red and enticing in the neglected orchard. 'Who gets the fruit?' he said at last, then left, with a few perfunctory words of advice, none too sympathetic. The question he had asked of no one in particular seemed somehow profound and resonant. I have never forgotten it, and even now will occasionally pronounce it, à propos of nothing, to the puzzlement of all. Who gets the fruit indeed?

But now the little money we had was running out. It became necessary to earn, or at any rate get, some money to live on. We went to London, picking up our few possessions in Oxford on the way, and began living from hand to mouth in Chelsea, moving from one bed-sitter to another, often in different parts of Oakley Street, another of those streets of which it was said that everybody in the world lived there at one time or another. There were times when we had no money at all. We became expert in the well-known trick of lying on the floor when landlords, milkmen or other creditors called, scarcely breathing as they hammered on the door and shouted through the letter-box like cops in a film: 'I know you're in there!' All sources of borrowing temporarily exhausted, we spent three whole days without eating, drinking only water. It was an interesting experience. After two days a certain light-headedness set in. We began drawing food on sheets of paper: chops, plates of bacon and eggs, a magnificent game pie.

Later on somebody gave us a few bits of elementary furniture and we rented an unfurnished room. I spent an interesting morning in the public library studying all the laws on distraint until I burst out laughing and the lady librarian hissed 'Quiet, please!' It seemed that bailiffs wishing to 'effect entry' into your premises were not allowed to force their way in; but if they found a window or skylight ever so slightly open they could enlarge the opening and so get inside. When distraining on goods and chattels they were obliged to leave the bare necessities: bed, chair, table, frying-pan, kettle, mug, plate, knife, fork and spoon. They could not remove the essential tools of a man's trade, which meant that my solid old black portable typewriter was safe. They were obliged to leave parrots (to give an example from the section about pets) an adequate supply of seed. They could not remove animals if by so doing they might cause injury to the person or a breach of the peace – for example, they could not remove your horse from under you.

At one time I had a job in an antiquarian bookshop, the only job

I have ever had, I think, at which I was expected to keep regular hours; but after a few weeks I was sacked, partly because I could not make up parcels with the primitive brown paper and string then used and partly because I had been found by the proprietor, entertaining, quite innocently, as it happened, a young woman in the basement. But it might not have been innocent. The sort of people we associated with and belonged to (if we belonged anywhere) were what were then called Bohemians. Our sexual morals were what would now be called 'permissive' and have become commonplace.

Former friends at Oxford such as Eithne Wilkins, who moved in a more respectable world, recommended me to several publishers; two or three, and those not obscure, showed a strong interest in my novel; but it seemed to evaporate when I went to see them. The book was eventually published twenty years later in a shortened form; but alas! the shadows of surrealism and Kafka – bane of English writers in the Thirties – lie all too heavily on it.

My wife was now getting occasional work as an artist's model. One of those who employed her was a rich amateur, Gerald Reitlinger, who appears in Anthony Powell's early novels and is pilloried in Wyndham Lewis's *Apes of God*. He was to die, many years later, in a tragic way after the burning of his house and porcelain collection. He read my book, praised it highly and told my wife I should 'shake my shaggy locks' and write another. I set to work in another burst of energy but with less enthusiasm, and produced, in a very short time, about 40,000 words of a second, Kafka-free novel and sent it to one of the interested publishers. They praised its 'atmosphere', but ... well, it has never been completed and almost certainly never will be.

Poverty led us into absurd adventures. Visiting some friends at Oxford – there was a new generation there who seemed to me more agreeable in some ways than my own coevals – I overstayed my welcome. Finding I had nowhere to sleep I climbed through the window of a store-room. There was nothing in it except hundreds of orange-coloured paperback copies of Gollancz Left Book Club publications piled on the floor. It was a warm summer evening. Making a nest among the books I fell into a sound and – considering the nature of my bed – a curiously dreamless sleep. I left at dawn before the keeper of this high-piled granary of Leftist propaganda could arrive. Can this experience, working through my dreaming mind, have reinforced and confirmed for ever my already strongly right-wing views?

Meanwhile I tried to shake my shaggy locks and wrote short stories and articles. The first piece of writing I ever had printed and paid for was an article about Welsh nationalism. It appeared, oddly enough, in the *New Statesman*, which also gave me a few books to review ('Nothing over 7s. 6d., mind!' shouted Raymond Mortimer quietly, as I looked over the shelves). Kingsley Martin, the editor, asked me suspiciously, 'Are you sure these Welsh nationalists aren't Fascists?'

This interest in Welsh nationalism (I had been greatly moved and impressed when the writer and scholar Saunders Lewis, with two other unlikely and unviolent people, set fire to an RAF training school in Llŷn, the very extremity and refuge of Welsh Wales, whose language I had studied after a fashion) shows the kind of politics which attracted me at that time, when Europe was moving towards a war which was to make them seem temporarily irrelevant. At Oxford I had occasionally been to meetings of the Chestertonian Distributist Club. I was particularly impressed by Father Vincent MacNab, a saintly man so hostile to machinery that he had even made his own fountain-pen. Later, in London, the Social Credit or 'Greenshirt' journal, the *New English Weekly*, printed some of my short stories, though as its editor Philip Mairet, a pleasant, quiet, pallid man who suffered from intestinal rumblings, explained, it could not afford to pay me anything. Was he, I wondered, listening to his own words and the words of his stomach, as hungry as I was?

I had developed, partly because of my general loathing for 'progress' and technology – I can claim to have been what is now called, somewhat nauseatingly, a 'friend of the earth' thirty years before the Environment was invented – an extreme hatred of Communism which has never left me. I was, if there can be such a thing, a 'Tory anarchist', an admirer of Cobbett, Ferrand, Oastler, Parson Bull and the great Bishop Philpotts of Exeter, of the 'Young England' party and of all who spoke out in early Victorian years against the factory system and against the 'Manchester bagmen and their calico millennium'. There was something of this strain, of a return to 'rural values' in the early days of the Nazi party, deceptive though it proved to be; and (although I had no love for either, to say the least) I would, I suppose, have had to say that I preferred Hitler to Stalin. I certainly hoped for Franco's victory in Spain, and this, of course, did not endear me to the intellectuals of that time.

Among such people, adherence to the 'Red' or 'Republican cause' was unthinking and automatic. They thought (just as the corresponding people think now, in different contexts) that an apparently intelligent person like myself must be posing or trying to be annoying when he expressed opposing principles. They were, I think, genuinely incredulous that I should not at least pretend to be trying to join the International Brigade.

One evening I was in a pub in what came to be known as 'Fitzrovia' – The Wheatsheaf, to be exact, once famous as a favourite haunt of Dylan Thomas – when I found myself talking, for no particular reason, to a tall young man who was wearing a beret and smoking French cigarettes. He was also holding forth volubly about anything or nothing. He was Constantine FitzGibbon, a man who was to become a firm friend and a strong influence in my life, though he was in almost all ways the opposite of myself.

75

He was of the Anglo-Irish 'ascendancy' on his (divorced) father's side; patrician American on his mother's. He had been on a precocious 'grand tour' of Europe, learning French and German, frequenting Paris cafés and who knows what inconceivable places. He was rich – at least his mother was – and even though he was then only seventeen, already had what seemed to me an air of great sophistication. We took to each other at once, discovering that we liked the same kind of jokes and fantastical conversations – of which we both had an inexhaustible supply – that we were both fond of drinking and that we had, surprisingly, much the same political opinions. It had not taken him long to shed the 'fun-Communism' which had got him expelled from Wellington.

He also had a mistress, if not two, and was at that time living with one of them in a bed-sitter in Oakley Street not far away from us, though at the more expensive end. The four of us became great friends. It was not merely that I liked Constantine and that he liked me. He offered a glimpse of a world I had never entered – the world of the upper class whose members, even if they were passive and lacked initiative, which he at least certainly did not, yet had an absolute confidence that whatever others might be, they could be themselves, with the right of entry to any place they chose.

Constantine 'seemed to know everybody'. At any rate he knew people like Dylan Thomas, Nina Hamnett, William Empson and Norman Cameron, as well as Count Potocki, with his long fair hair and velvet cloak, the self-styled King of Poland, a person of extreme reactionary views who insisted on marching at the rear of Blackshirt demonstrations, greatly to the Mosleyites' embarrassment.

Under his tutelage I began to meet people I would certainly not have met otherwise, though it is true I did not feel comfortable with them, and tended to hover in batlike unease on the outer edges of their tremendous parties. All the same, I drank, laughed, talked agreeable nonsense. I even went to a few night-clubs and in the afternoons, to those most agreeable of drinking-clubs with very few customers, where, as the pianist tinkled away, I could sink into a mild alcoholic trance, as if into a feather-bed where I would be visited by the strangest dreams, glorified versions of those distortions of the real world seen through the many-coloured glass fanlights of childhood.

I was at the celebrated opening of the London Surrealist Exhibition, with its underwater piano and cup and saucer made of fur, when Dylan Thomas, after going round inserting various objects such as carrots and pencil-sharpeners by way of improving the exhibits, smashing a picture over some art critic's head and leaving the frame stuck round his neck, was eventually flung out. A very beautiful German countess, seeing me standing wistfully in a corner, declared that she was in love with me and invited me to call at her flat in Hammersmith next day. I did so but found there was no such address. Such idiocies were not uncommon. And there were occasions when I did wake up in women's beds uncertain of how I had got there. I also had that sinister experience, familiar to drinkers, of waking up alone in a strange room after a prolonged drinking bout, uncertain whether it was early morning or late evening and waiting for the light to fade or brighten as the case might be, and thus set my uneasy mind at rest.

I heard the chimes at midnight. But it would be misleading to describe my life at that time as totally worthless and disgraceful. It is no bad thing for a young man who is going to be a writer or any sort of artist to spend a few years of his youth doing nothing in particular, except absorb impressions both from life and books. One day, in the Chelsea public library, I came by chance on Rimbaud's *Illuminations*, borrowed it and read those magical prose poems over and over again in transports of delight. I had never before come across any writing which gave me so exactly what I wanted. My wife had been away for a few days, perhaps trying to raise money from her relations; when she got back she could not make out what on earth had happened to me. She assumed I had fallen in love, as in a sense I had.

Another 'seminal' book I read about this time was *Mystics and Magicians in Tibet*, by Alexandra David-Neel, the first European woman to enter Lhasa, who died in 1969 at the age of 100. I was fascinated by her account of life in Tibetan monasteries, the festivals, devil-dances, exhibitions of butter sculpture; the annual psychic sports, when the monks would compete in levitation, in moving objects at a distance (or telekinesis as it is now called), in the production of thought-forms, and in the generation of supernatural body heat, where the competitors had to strip and sit naked in the snow all night, the monk who melted the largest patch of snow being the winner.

There were the splendid ceremonials, when the great nobles and abbots appeared in their ritual garments of silk, brocade and gold; at the New Year, at the beginning of February, there were the epileptic writhings and obscure pronouncements of the State Oracle before the assembled multitude. All was unchanging ritual, an unchanging hierarchy from high to low. Whether I believed every word – or even many of the words – of Mme David-Neel's highly wrought account, it seemed then – as it seems now – to portray a most satisfactory form of what is boringly called social organisation. There were only two possible answers to any query: 'It is the custom', or 'It is not the custom'. Life in Tibet was harsh, cold and uncomfortable, even for the rich. The peasants were poor and unimaginably dirty, but – other travellers and witnesses confirmed this – they seemed always to be smiling. If they stank, they stank of happiness.

Now it has all gone, destroyed by the Communist Chinese conquerors (or, perhaps, rightly regarded, from a Tibetan viewpoint, it is all still there). I have read many books about Tibet since then. But I am grateful to Mme David-Neel. Apart from influencing my 'political ideas', her book gave me for several nights a series of coloured dreams which I have never forgotten; even after all these years they can still flood my mind with wonder.

My political ideas, indeed! Could they or can they be called ideas? Chiefly they amount to no more than a conviction that in the age I have lived in all change is for the worse. It is said that anyone who is not a Socialist at the age of twenty has no heart and that anyone who is not a Conservative at the age of forty is a fool. I have always been a Conservative. I have always hated 'progress'. I have always been a pessimist.

Now the wandering psychologist I have occasionally mentioned might well say that I held these opinions because of a reaction against myself and my own character and antecedents. A person of contradictory background, both of race and class, a person without roots, unsure of his own place in the world, I ought by rights to have been a rabid revolutionary, bent on destroying our existing society. Instead, I was a passionate upholder of the status quo; a passionate defender of the very people, the middle and upper class, with whom, a few excepted, I could never feel at ease and who, perhaps for that reason, had little time for me.

A person of melancholy, retiring nature, I most admired those who were exactly the opposite – outgoing, sanguine, confident. Lacking in self-esteem, I admired those who stood up for themselves, particularly against the odds (the White Rhodesians and South Africans were to prove good examples later on). Above all, I would choose the losing side, and there at least, as an instinctive loser, I had a kind of consistency. No wonder I supported Franco when all my generation held him in execration; and even felt a perverse sympathy with the Nazis and the Italian fascists. They may have looked like winners in 1937. But I knew that they, with all they stood for, were doomed to be defeated. If I was a passionate anti-Communist, it was partly because I felt that Communism was going to win, that in various forms and guises the barbarians, the materialists, the atheists, the levellers, the worshippers of perverted science, the destroyers of hierarchy and ritual splendour would take over the world – though not, of course, for ever. To believe that would be ultimate despair.

Irreligious by nature, with no more than a social parody of a Christian upbringing, I have always hankered after the unchanging certainty of the Roman Catholic faith as it was before the Second Vatican Council destroyed it. But for that I should undoubtedly have been a Catholic. Would it have been its rituals, incense and sonorous Latin that attracted me? Not entirely. Still unable to believe in the essential Christian doctrines – the Incarnation and Redemption – I know, all the same, that this is not the only world there is.

Was it, the wandering psychiatrist would wonder, 'merely' awareness of my own irreligious nature that made me disbelieve in the supremely irreligious Marxist concept of Heaven on Earth? Was it, to some extent, awareness of having Jewish blood which made me reject, with horror and outrage, that secular, 'Jewish' vision of the future? It might be so. But even if it were so, that would not mean, of course, that I was wrong to reject it.

This is a digression, perhaps a confusing one. I cannot remember much discussion of political or religious matters among my friends at that time. We were mostly intent on enjoying ourselves before the deluge. Constantine was due to go to Oxford in the autumn of 1937. In the meantime, like many young people of his class and habits of life, he decided, that summer, that it would be a good idea to go and live in the South of France with his current or principal mistress. So off they went to Cassis, near Marseilles. It was arranged that we should join them there. But whether owing to my habitual torpor, or lack of money for the fare (life in France at that time was, of course, incredibly cheap for English or American people), or a feeling that actually to 'go abroad' was something which so far exceeded my low expectations in life as to be out of the question, we stayed in London, still living from hand to mouth and moving from one lodging to another.

There were other friends to replace Constantine and his associates, most of whom we did not really fit in with. There was David Thomson, my friend of Oxford days, involved, though I did not know it then, in a hopeless love affair in Ireland which he was to make, years afterwards, into a fine book marred only by a misleading though typically generous view of Irish history. Alan Davis turned up from time to time, as poor as we were or even poorer, living I know not how or where, but still a figure of magic. On the tin whistle he was a virtuoso. He could play not only the two octaves of its normal range but also in what he called the 'spectral tone', an eerie sound he had discovered by experiment. It seemed to come from another world. I was a fair player myself and we used to play duets, mainly Scottish airs such as 'Ye Banks and Braes o' Bonnie Doon', with quite ravishing effect. We occasionally played for money in the street, mainly in the Fulham Road on rainy nights, when we collected a few pennies but were not a great success.

We decided to write a bestseller and set to work industriously, writing alternate chapters. It was a preposterous romance about a Welsh colony on an island somewhere in the Pacific, with a beautiful heroine called Branwen and assorted cardboard characters such as 'the ticket-of-leave man, Ransom', heroic, self-sacrificing Ifan Cadwallader-Jones, the villainous Dr Crevasse and others. It was, of course, hopelessly unpublishable. Alan, partly from having a practical, even surprisingly cynical streak ('all that fuss about a bitch in a black dress') and partly from unreliability, gave up half-way, leaving me to complete the remaining chapters in a dogged, obstinate, masochistic way. Sheets of this ghastly romance, which I typed out in triplicate, kept turning up even twenty years afterwards and were useful for writing on the back of.

Alan had new surrealist hymns to sing to us, too. Here is one, perhaps the longest fragment still remaining in my memory:

'The singing of the dentist's wife,
As I lay in my bunk,
Brought me fresh liberty and life,
Though she was rotten drunk . . .

I saw His boots, I saw His feet,
I chased Him all down Oxford Street,
I dined with Him at Marble Arch
On damson shillebeer and starch.

He is the shout, the victory
By thirteen goals to nil;
Moly and febrifuge is He
When folks are taken ill . . .'

There was also a beautiful song which began:

'Back in the old village band,
With a lemon cheese tart in my hand . . .'

The rest is lost, unless by chance some survivor of those days who knew this strange and wonderful man can supply more, and help, perhaps, to produce the memoir he deserves.

It was now clear to all except the blind and deaf that war was not far off. We got used to hearing, with a kind of horrid fascination, the voice of the Führer on the wireless as he went into the *hwyl* – I had a theory that he was really a Welshman, an Alpine Celt such as the Nazi racial theorist Rosenberg might have dreamed of in an unguarded moment – and the disciplined howling of his people. The Sudeten Germans came into the news; Czechoslovakia, a distant country of which I knew something – that it was an artificial creation – was now the object of Hitler's attention. He declared or was said to have declared that it was his last.

Now came conscription, slit-trenches in the parks, sandbag-filling, gas-mask-fitting in Chelsea Town Hall, hard by the old Six Bells and Bowling Green where I had so often sat joking and fantasticating, or on days when we could afford only one glass of beer, drooping listlessly and watching the old men who had 'been in the last lot' at their bowls. And now came fear.

Another factor had entered our lives. My wife and I had dis-covered, some time in the year before, how to make love properly and she was promptly pregnant. The baby, a boy, was born in February, a healthy specimen enough. Thanks to the bounty and help of a woman doctor, a friend of one of my cousins, the only member of my family, apart from my parents, whom I was still on terms with – and that not for long – Nicholas was born in a nursing-home in Putney and duly came home with his mother to a flea-ridden, barely furnished flat somewhere near the Fulham Road. It is worth mentioning that I had not told my parents of my marriage at the time, nor did I tell them of the baby's birth until it became impossible or pointless to conceal it.

It was at this time, in any case, that I decided to 'make a new start in life', not precisely to 'go straight' or 'become respectable', but to become more responsible, soundly based and honest, now that I was a father. One step I took, to assume my maternal name of Wharton, may seem to some people to be dishonest rather than honest. But I did not think so then and I do not think so now. I wanted to escape once and for all from the oddity and even absurdity of my early life and one symbolic way of doing this was to remove a label which did not suit me or, quite apart from its immense potency in the eyes of others, rightly belong to me. Years later my son, himself one of the reasons for the change, decided, in a burst of Jewish romanticism at the time of the Israeli victory in the Six Days War, to change his name back, though in fact it belongs to him even less, by precisely half, than it belongs to me. 'Would you', he asked me, 'really rather belong to generations of English North Country clod-hoppers and dolts or even landowning bullies and villains than to the ancient people of Heine, to say nothing of the people of Goethe and Beethoven?' I thought for a long time about this, then answered 'Yes.' But of course it was neither a straight question nor a straight answer. Having no choice, I belong to all these disparate worlds at once.

When the baby was born, we decided, like a lot of people, that London was not a good place to be. 'If there is another war,' people had been saying ever since I could remember, particularly old men in the West Riding, where they knew everything, 'if there is another war, we' – and they obviously thought *they* would survive whatever happened – 'shall all be living in caves afterwards.' Because the First World War was not all that long ago – in fact the Second, as it turned out, was merely the continuation of it – the terror of another war was probably much greater than it is now, nuclear weapons and all, after nearly forty years of peace in Europe. Most people believed that London and other cities would be obliterated within hours ('the bomber will always get through') and that poison gas would be used immediately on the largest possible scale.

If we were not exactly heroic, we were not alone in that. Nor did I believe, before the Nazi-Soviet Pact of August 1939, that it was our necessary duty to go to war with Germany, or, after the German invasion of the Soviet Union in 1941, to prosecute such a war to the point of Germany's total destruction and the partition of Germany and Europe. With hindsight, I now believe it even less, knowing what I then only guessed from hints and rumours, that there were men and women in Germany who, if they had been given due support, might have overthrown Hitler and the murderous gang who had imposed their odious system on a great nation. This was not a popular view of things then, nor is it, strangely enough, acceptable even now, when we know so much more of the truth about both Nazi Germany and Soviet Russia. But I am not ashamed of it. If it had prevailed, how different our unfortunate country and the whole world might be now! Such speculations, of course, were and are completely futile.

After Munich we left London and moved into a cottage I had found, after some false trails, a few miles from Appleby in the valley of the Eden in Westmorland, in that bounteous region I had glimpsed years before in my wanderings along the summits of the barren Pennines from my brother's farm at Fell End. It had looked like paradise then and so, in a curious way, it was to prove.

The county of Westmorland had long been endeared to me in a hundred ways, in particular the Valley of the Eden. I remembered, in a half-mocking way, my mother's hints, gradually turning into positive belief, that her father's people had come from there. And wasn't Wharton Hall, seat of a once powerful family, only a few miles further up the valley, near Kirkby Stephen, whose red sandstone church even had a Wharton Chapel, with recumbent effigies of the first Lord Wharton and his two wives? The Hall itself was ruined now, its courtyard, chapel, great hall, terrace and parapets incorporated into a farmhouse. Perhaps the Missing Will itself was hidden somewhere in its ivied crannies? And, as a voice from Shipley said in a flat North Midland accent quite different from the sharp, attractive sing-song of the Westmorland people, who spoke a true North-Western dialect: 'Aye, and perhaps not.'

There were certainly plenty of people called Wharton in the neighbourhood where we settled. But none of them claimed relationship with the great family of the Hall; nor, I suppose, did they claim relationship, however distant, with myself. Yet I felt at home in the Valley of the Eden. Our cottage, I felt, was the first settled home I had ever had, and I cherished every part of it.

We had moved in, with a few bits of furniture and books – chiefly the twenty-four volumes of the *Encyclopaedia Britannica* and my well-loved typewriter which had been through so much – at the end of 1938 and awoke on New Year's Day, a fine, frosty morning, loud with the baby's cries, in a dank house quickly drying out with the enormous fires we had lit in every grate. I stepped out on to the narrow flagged pathway outside the front door, feeling dejected for myself and apprehensive for my wife and baby in the uncertain future. But the sun was coming up gloriously on the right hand above the flat top of Wildboar Fell. I felt reassured as we had our first breakfast and arranged our small effects.

The rent of this quite roomy cottage was 10s. a month. It had no electric light and only one cold water tap, connected to the mains for our arrival. It had a huge copper in one of its capacious kitchens for washing clothes and taking baths. Hordes of migrant rats visited it at intervals, some of them big enough to defy the big brindled cat a neighbouring farmer's wife produced, struggling in a sack, soon after we moved in ('Ye'll be wantin' this, I'se reckon').

Some nights we could hear these rats scampering overhead; it was as if they were holding sports meetings or even moving their rat-furniture about. I got quite fond of them. One particular rat I had got to recognise would come quite close, staring at me without fear with its bright eyes as I sat reading about Ballistics or the Punic Wars by the light of four candles stuck in those cheap round tin candleholders which must then have been counted in millions throughout England. Where are they all now? They have the curious pathos of things, once familiar to everybody, which all at once vanish from memory.

One of the chief subjects of discussion at the small pub about half a mile away through the fields was the best way of catching rats. Some recommended long planks placed against the wainscot ('he likes a tunnel, like, to run along, dosta see?') with a trap at the end. Others suggested elaborate devices involving cardboard boxes, balanced weights and pails of water. Others believed in poisoned sandwiches ('cut triangular. He likes 'em all dainty, like'). But I was not too keen on catching them at all. One night later on, a friend who was staying with us went to bed early with his supper – a pint of beer and a pilchard sandwich, a great standby for cheapness and nourishment. He fell asleep and woke with a scream to find a big rat dragging the sandwich off his chest. We thought this very funny at the time.

What did we live on? Well, I had discovered about the time we left London that as well as doing 'serious' writing, which brought in hardly any money (though I did get a short story called 'The Bitter Lozenge' – an unkind bit of writing based on 'Aunt' and her herb book – published in the very first issue of Cyril Connolly's *Horizon*), I discovered I had a knack of writing short pieces of humorous fantasy for which *Punch* was willing to pay about £12 a thousand words. I sent these off to London most weeks under the pseudonym 'Simon Crabtree', often writing them at night, with the rats' eyes on me, at the last possible moment for next week's issue – it was often almost as bad as writing essays for my Oxford tutorials, but at least they were paid for – bicycling into Appleby next morning to post them and then, with great relief, do some shopping and drink a pint of beer.

With its broad, sloping main street, the Castle at the top, the Moot Hall down below and St Lawrence's Church at the bottom, and its fine, solid houses, Appleby, the county town of Westmorland, was and still is, for all the cars that choke it now, one of the most perfect and delightful little market towns in England. In those days Lord Hothfield, a big, tall man, every inch a Peer of the Realm, still lived in the Castle. He was, I think, perpetual mayor – who would have ventured to oppose him? – and an imposing figure in the mayoral procession at times of the Assizes, when the Judge invariably got his traditional pair of white gloves since there were never any cases to be tried.

There were nine pubs in Appleby to choose from. I generally took my pint of beer either in The Crown and Cushion or in The Hare and Hounds on the opposite side of the main street. I sometimes had a game of dominoes in The Crown and Cushion, where there were regular habitués whose faces and names I have forgotten, though they sometimes detained me with beer and dominoes longer than I had meant to stay. If I was not feeling particularly sociable I went to The Hare and Hounds, where I was usually the only customer. The landlord, a taciturn elderly man, was also a carpenter. After he had drawn my pint from the barrel he would retire to his back yard, leaving me alone in the stone-flagged, barely furnished room to drink my beer and listen to the sound of his sawing and hammering. What was he making? A coffin, I imagined. It went well with his grave manner. And sometimes his equally taciturn and elderly wife would come and sit by the fire without speaking, knitting away at what must surely have been a shroud.

On something like £30 a month my wife and I and the baby could live quite easily. My wife was a good manager, with what I called a very high 'nidification index' – that is, she was expert at converting the bare cottage into a simple but comfortable home. She could sew both curtains and cushions. She sometimes went to auction sales, returning with amazing bargains – a small sofa, a fine scrubbed table, wheel-backed chairs, rugs. Idle though I was by nature, I did my best to live up to my new role. There was quite a big plot of garden in front of the house, looking across the valley towards the Northern Pennines and the flat top of Crossfell. Here I set to, with my gleaming new spade, to dig up the whole plot. I worked at this for two hours on most mornings, taking about two months to turn over an area which an expert digger – or even an average one – would have managed in a week – even allowing for the frequent pauses I made, resting on my spade, looking with pleasure at the woods and hills and watching the numerous birds which began to appear as the year advanced and spring came on – greenfinches, bullfinches, goldfinches. Once, I convinced myself I had seen a pair of hawfinches, largest and rarest of their tribe.

Then came planting, seeding the strip of ground by the flagged path in front of the house with a few simple flowers and the rest with rows of potatoes, cabbages, carrots, onions and turnips. To my amazement – I had never grown anything before – these, or most of them, actually came up. We lived quite well. I shot an occasional rabbit with my airgun. Nettles, when young and green, are at least as agreeable as spinach. A friendly gamekeeper, whom I occasionally drank with at the pub, would sometimes leave a brace of pheasant hanging on the back door, where we would find them when we got up. One habit we kept from earlier days was late rising.

As spring advanced we began to explore the neighbourhood, propelling the often complaining baby along rough tracks in his push-chair. Soon he began to crawl, then stand up in his play-pen, pushing it round the room and in this way learning to walk. Most interesting was the development of his speech. All infants, before they learn to copy the 'recognised pronunciation' of their parents, construct their own phonetic system and follow its rules for a time with inner consistency. This baby's temporary phonetic system was unusually elaborate.

He could not pronounce words beginning with a sibilant followed by another consonant, so he used nasals in their place. For 'spade' he said 'made'; for 'stone' 'none'. I did an experiment, asking him to repeat the word 'skate', and sure enough out came a perfect 'ngate'. I wrote this down and my wife said she couldn't pronounce it. I was sorry when this individual phonetic system, which even produced 'mlice' for 'splice', disappeared. But later, when, knowing the words 'bee' and 'motor', the child looked up at an aeroplane overhead – a rarity, even a troubling portent – and at once cried 'motor bee' I began to think we had produced a prodigy.

This was a dreamlike time which now seems one of undiluted bliss. It was not, of course; I had not ceased, even in Westmorland, to be a state-registered melancholiac, and even in that spring and summer, particularly in wet weather, would have black moods which lasted for days on end, as I sat in our only armchair with closed eyes, refusing to speak, while my patient, sensible wife went busily about her tasks. Such moods might sometimes be resolved by bouts of love-making. But not always or even very often. I did not love my extremely lovable wife as I should have done, hankering foolishly after girls more beautiful, more strange, more eccentric or even – ultimate stupidity on my part – more clever.

But the summer of 1939 was fine (or was it? we can take it that it was) and while the news from the outside world crackled more and more violently and threateningly from our wireless set we were, on the whole, happy enough in what was then an escapist's dream, a really sequestered part of England, with hardly a car on the roads and not a single tractor in the fields. On many mornings we would cook and eat our breakfast out of doors, either in our orchard, which grew not only apple trees but the finest damson trees, the local women said, in all Westmorland, or by the small, stony, strong-running beck – there was a kingfisher there – a couple of fields away from our cottage.

We were all the more happy – or so it seems now – because we knew that very soon – one year, two years? – this kind of life must have an end. We had felt something like panic just before Munich, and a momentary relief – after all, we were not professional politicians – when the Prime Minister returned with 'peace in our time'. We knew very well that there was not going to be peace in our time. But in a curious way (I can speak only for myself) I had worked the fear out of my system at the time of Munich, and when, eleven months later, the next and final 'crisis' came, it did not return. I even had moments of bravado, quoting from my favourite Yeats, whose strange, much-derided book *A Vision* I read over and over again, that message from his spirit communicators: 'Dear predatory birds, prepare for war. Prepare your children and all that you can reach . . .'

That last summer of the old world the beauty of the countryside intoxicated me. When I was not doing my weekly money-making stint for *Punch* or other 'serious' writings which for the most part have never been completed or seen the light of day except in transmogrified form, reading the Encyclopaedia from A to Z, not necessarily in that order, tending the garden, playing with the baby or otherwise employed, I spent whole days alone, on foot or bicycle, exploring near and far. There were moments of that paradisial experience which Wordsworth knew; whose gradual loss he mourned; that feeling of the numinous I had always known since childhood, but now intensified and prolonged to the point of ecstasy. Now that it has utterly gone from me – or is it waiting somewhere to be retrieved? – it is hard even to believe in the sweet, enormous joy which seized me in those luminous evenings of May.

On one such evening I stood in the winding, stony lane which led from the main road to our cottage; the soft, suffused light of the sun going down, the smell of may blossom, the calling of birds, the rustle, almost imperceptible, of the trees and tall grasses by the wayside filled me with serene delight. I leaned on my bicycle, waiting for my wife to come from our cottage to meet me, and thought: supposing it were some girl I truly loved, as I loved with holy fervour this natural world spread about me on every side! That would have been a perfection of life in which the erotic and the numinous, the human and the inhuman, would have been joined together in an experience I have never known. Not having known it, have I ever lived? Did she repine, as I did, at the incomplete beauty of such evenings? Was that why there was nothing to say as I laid my bicycle on the verge and we walked on with a sense of something lost or missing, never to be attained?

However, there were many consolations. Who that has sat, when young, in an outside privy in Westmorland on a fine June morning, with the door wide open, watching the procession of the clouds across the sky and listening to the songs of the birds, with a big slice of currant pasty in his hand, can say that he has never lived?

Friends from London or elsewhere would sometimes arrive

without warning, but there was room enough for all, provided they did not mind the rats and scarcity of washing arrangements. Alan Davis stayed for a few days in the course of a pilgrimage he was making to Iona on a borrowed motorbike. It was the last time I was to set eyes on this extraordinary man.

One afternoon, to our amazement, Constantine FitzGibbon came loping down our lane. He had left Oxford, quarrelled with his rich mother and was temporarily 'penniless', a comparative term. We agreed that time was short. Hitler ranted nightly about the provocations of the Poles, while we talked, drank, gathered mushrooms in the fields (it goes without saying that there was a stupendous crop of them that year), played darts or dominoes in the pub and discussed the situation with men whose views and opinions, still to a large extent their own and not imposed by centralised 'media', were often, to say the least, strange and far-fetched.

This pub was a small, narrow building with a kitchen at one end from which, on many mornings, came the delicious smell of baking, and two tiny bars, the larger given over to darts and dominoes. It smelt of generations of beer-drinking. To enter it was like going inside a rich plumcake. Every man in it was what would now be called a 'character', from the landlord, an edentate man with slight sadistic tendencies, to the various farmers, labourers and gamekeepers, each with his own peculiarity. There was a good deal of the rustic humour which cannot have changed since the middle ages – verbal jokes which would seem innocent enough in our time of electronic pornography, and practical jokes of immemorial antiquity, such as tying a curly pig's tail to a man's coat – a slightly 'simple' man called Frank was usually the victim. There was also a mythological cycle about a local character nicknamed 'Wufflicote' because of his tousled, Old English sheepdog appearance, an elderly man (I suppose he was about forty) who was notorious for prop-ositioning women, invariably without success, though this did not save him, later on, from a well-deserved beating from some local girl's brother. 'Wufflicote' had once appeared at our door when I was away on one of my rambles, and when my wife appeared, at once offered to mend an undamaged slate on the roof. He did not get inside, but the incident, I suppose, was incorporated in the mythological cycle, decorated and expanded. It was all very harmless and amusing.

On Saturday evenings we would walk, either by road or by the field path which led over the beck, through Bandley Wood – favourite resort of lovers – and past the brand-new Observer Corps post into Appleby. To make a ritual pub crawl, we were obliged to drink in each of its nine pubs – not only The Crown and Cushion and The Hare and Hounds, but The Tufton Arms, the principal inn of the town, with its Crimean War daguerrotypes and slightly superior air (it closed its doors at times of the New Fair in June, when knife-carrying gypsies and other troublemakers were about), The Golden Ball, The Chequers, The Aboard, which was so narrow that only one man could enter it at a time, The King's Head by the river, The Grapes, The Royal Oak in Bongate, haunt of malignant dwarfs, and even the gloomy Railway Inn, where even on the finest evenings a gritty feeling, brought all the way from London, seemed to lurk.

Towards the end of August Constantine came to stay with a new, delightful girl whom, as so often, I coveted myself, but in a way so obviously hopeless that the friendship of the four of us was not marred. News came that the Nazis had signed their pact with the Russian Communists. To us, as to Evelyn Waugh, this was a kind of relief. War was now certain and until 1941 it was to be, beyond question, a war against the right enemies, a conjunction of evil monsters; in Waugh's own phrase, we 'faced the modern world in arms'.

We woke on the morning of Friday, 1 September to the news that the Germans had invaded Poland. Two strange days of waiting followed. I doubt if we were ever entirely sober. There was a great deal of love-making too; there is nothing like a 'crisis', a feeling of excitement and apprehension, to induce a state of priapism. The political discussions in the pub, which we visited as often as there was time to spare, became more and more outlandish; one man thought the danger was not so much from the Germans (whom he had fought in what was still 'the War') as the Japanese. He maintained, looking up uneasily at the sky for weird oriental-looking planes, that they were importing into England large quantities of extra-strong mint imperials, which, when swallowed, would explode inside you, not violently enough to blow you to bits, but enough to make you fall downstairs or stagger into the road and be run over by a lorry. 'They're coonnin' devils, tha knaws,' he said. He claimed, when the landlady, a magnificent Westmorland woman with the face of one of the better Roman emperors, put a finger to her forehead, to have seen one of these diabolical sweets in a pub in Penrith. 'Didst eat it, then?' 'Nay, they'se noan catchin' me that way.'

There were troops moving on the roads; there was a rumour that parachutists, not yet the sort disguised as nuns, had already landed at such key points as Crosby Ravensworth and Temple Sowerby; a strange blue light had been seen over at Keisley, away on the other side of Appleby, where the helm wind sometimes blew; an unpopular old lady in another part of the county was said to have hedges in her garden in the form of a swastika, unrecognisable from the ground but useful for the Luftwaffe. Not only that, but she was said to have a Nazi flag all ready in her linen cupboard. Even my own addiction to apparently motiveless bicycling and my collection of large-scale maps of the district came in for teasing accusations of espionage and, later on, brought a visit from the police, tipped off, some thought, by the disappointed 'Wufflicote'.

By night, marring that perfect darkness which nobody can ever see in England now, searchlights appeared far away over the

Pennines, guarding the north-eastern coasts, as good a sign as any that our private paradise was lost. And so, at noon on that fine morning of Sunday, 3 September 1939, we listened to its death-sentence in the voice of Mr Neville Chamberlain, hoarse, paper-thin yet determined, sounding more disappointed than angry, from our ancient wireless-set: '. . . consequently this country is at war with Germany . . . it is not the German people . . . but evil things we shall be fighting against . . .' I am told that in a burst of inverted bravado I declared I would go to bed and stay there till the war was over. But that was not the way things turned out at all.

3
Saluting on the March

I did not go to bed 'for the duration', but unlike Constantine, who left very soon to join the Irish Guards, while his girl enlisted in the Women's Auxiliary Air Force, I carried on through the 'Phoney War' and the summer that followed, awaiting my call up in an unheroic manner. When the Russian Communists invaded Finland and there was talk of forming a British Expeditionary Force to help the Finns, I wrote to the War Office to inquire about volunteering. But nothing came of that. It was naive of me to think (if I really did) that when the Russian Communists, as arranged by their pact with the Nazis, occupied large parts of Poland, the country on whose behalf we had ostensibly gone to war, we should automatically have declared war, or at least been in a 'state of war' with Communist Russia as well as Nazi Germany. What a glorious, noble, quixotic war that would have been – and what a gloriously hopeless one! Or would it have been hopeless? We cannot tell how events would have interacted and alliances reshaped themselves.

We went on with our usual pursuits. Apart from some night-scented stock beneath our windows, the garden grew only vegetables that year. I went on writing my articles for *Punch*; I went on playing dominoes in The Crown and Cushion and meditating on mortality in The Hare and Hounds; I bought a map of Europe and some pins to stick in it; one fine spring day, which we had spent lazily by the beck side, we returned to the cottage to find that the Nazis had invaded Denmark and Norway; I could now begin to stick in my pins and, next month, on another beautiful day, I had need of a fresh supply. The Nazis had begun their blitzkrieg in the West and the real war had begun.

My call-up papers arrived. Anticipating matters, I went to Carlisle and enlisted in the Royal Artillery, thereby ensuring that I should know the precise date of my call-up and have a short time to put my affairs in order, as the saying is. My affairs were few and soon put in order. On a gloomy late afternoon in November I took leave of my wife and child, and bidding them stay in the cottage, walked along the winding lane for what I supposed might be the last time. As I stood waiting for the bus which was to take me to Tebay Junction (as I lived in Westmorland, the Army had arranged for me to begin my training in Exeter), our friend the gamekeeper joined me. He remarked, as well he might, on the suitcase I had with me, which was to be used, as Army regulations laid down, for returning my civilian clothes. It was a heavy leather suitcase which had belonged to my father and was stuck all over with the labels of foreign hotels – the Hotel Bristol in Dresden, the Elephant at Zagreb, the Grand Hotel at Riga and so on – all symbols of that Europe which was now to be destroyed.

I broke my journey and stayed that night at Shrewsbury, clinging, I suppose, to my status as civilian to the last and next day watching to the last the passing fields and woods of Herefordshire, where I had walked and bicycled only a few years before. When the train arrived at Exeter I had ceased to be a civilian and had become one of the month's intake at Topsham Barracks, to sleep that night with my fellow-recruits in the old stables, to shave and wash in cold water next morning as best I could and then spend several days being classified, numbered, documented, issued with various items of uniform, medically and dentally checked, intelligence-tested and absorbed into what might have been called the 'military machine'. But machine was just what it was not.

The most unmilitary of men, I had assumed that I should spend my career in the Army, if I was kept in it at all, cleaning latrines, collecting and sorting waste paper and performing various humble tasks of that sort under the bulging eyes of ferocious NCOs, lashed by their pitiless tongues. It was not so. I made several discoveries in that first week. One was that in any representative group of men, such as an Army squad, there will always be one or two who are quite easy to get along with. Another discovery was that life in the Army – at any rate as a Gunner – was hilariously funny. What could be funnier, to begin with, than being known as '1083777 Gunner Wharton MB'?

That first month of marching, counter-marching, turning right, turning left, saluting on the march, with rifles or without, of PT on the chilly playing fields with the soft woods and hills of Devon to look at – I had never before been in the West Country – now seems like a comic dream. Quite a lot of the men in my squad came from the slums of Liverpool and had never left them before. Their incessant, monotonous use of the common expletives was comical in itself. Comical was their bewilderment at the train journey from Liverpool to Exeter ('animals in the fields – miles and miles of fuck all'); comical were their stories of life in Liverpool, with its gruesome incidents of German bombs, its larger than life characters, the mere mention of whose names, as with my own family, was enough to raise tremendous guffaws ('Farting Liza! Remember those pies she made out of old tram tickets?'): all this was novel and fascinating.

This worked both ways. The green pyjamas I wore when we kipped down on our blankets on the floor around the glowing coke-stove in the Nissen hut were a matter of wonder to my fellow gunners rather than scorn. My way of talking, far from being an offence, was also a matter of wonder. If I had worn spectacles I should have been called 'Prof.'. As it was that nickname was reserved for a former schoolmaster, the one man in our squad who took everything with deadly seriousness and was therefore thought much more odd and even ridiculous than I was. The spirit of class deference was still gloriously alive in England. I was its unworthy beneficiary.

We were a very mixed lot. But in those early days we had one overriding interest. No, it was not beating Hitler and suppressing the Nazis. I doubt if I ever heard, either then or later, any such sentiments expressed. There may have been soldiers who talked in such Churchillian terms. If so, I did not meet them. There was merely a sense of being part of a great Necessity, whose purpose, neither questioned nor spoken of, was to prevent our country from being changed by foreigners, whoever they might be, into something different from what it was. There was a great and wonderful innocence about these men, an absence of envy and mean class hatred. There were those, as I know now, who saw in the war a means of changing that innocence and decency and to a large extent succeeded.

Our overriding interest, in those early days, was to put a fantastic shine on our boots. This, our sergeant, a handsome, smart-looking Irishman, had indicated, was a primary duty in that first month. He gave several hints, such as the use of bones, on how this was to be done. There was great competition for shining our boot-caps 'till you could see to shave in them', and although the word 'bullshit' was often used, nobody, except a few amiable, illiterate men already earmarked for transfer to the Pioneer Corps, thought of not competing. One or two of us, who had more money than the private soldier's 10s. a week (about 7s. 6d. after deductions for haircuts and 'barrack-room damages') paid the odd sixpence to a wizened, elderly recruit (I suppose he was about thirty-five) to keep polishing away at our boots so that we could spend more time drinking beer and eating chips in the Naafi while listening to Gunner Harrison tinkling out tunes on the cigarette-blistered piano. The elderly recruit had formerly been in the army of what was then the neutral Irish Free State. He could hardly believe in the sybaritic comfort, lavish pay and generally 'cushy' conditions of the British Army.

I do not think my boots, even with this Irishman's help, were the shiniest of all, but they would pass. My buttons, too, thanks to hours with Brasso and button-stick, were reasonably bright. My kit, laid out for Saturday morning inspection in a rigidly traditional pattern which gave me, a natural Tibetan, intense pleasure, was as satisfactory as the next man's. Once, forewarned in a dream that the metal rings round our water-bottle corks would be the object of special attention (this was technically called 'a blitz on water-bottle corks'), I earned good marks from the inspecting officer for being the only man who had thought of polishing this most obscure item of equipment. My fellow-recruits (we were yet far from being soldiers) did not mind. They had learned to take an interest in my dreams. As we lay, dog-tired after a day's drill, round the stove in our hut, the snoring and groaning – it was Rayner Heppenstall, another literary recruit then training somewhere else in England, but less cunning and adaptable than I was, who wrote the memorable line, 'I hear the khaki beast grieve in his stall' – this collective bombination would sometimes take an articulate form. One man habitually sang hymns in his sleep and was cursed for it. I sometimes shouted out: 'I did not do it! I tell you I did not do it! I am innocent!' Next morning my comrades would ask me, with wonder, almost with admiration, 'But what *did* you do, mate? It must have been something fuckin' terrible.' They may have been right.

Although I was inclined to flat feet and tended to clash my rifle against my tin hat when marching with rifle at the slope, I enjoyed the drill, while grumbling with the rest at being spilled out from warm and frowsty beds on to the vast barrack-square at an hour when the stars were not yet fading in the sky. I liked the ritual patterns and was particularly good at 'rhythm' drill, when only parts of the words of command were shouted out and our feet had to complete the correct movements of this leaden yet fast-moving dance.

I even liked the nights when I was on sentry-duty ('eight hours on and eight hours off') with its ritual of changing guard; and once claimed, when I had been on duty at the main gate of the barracks, that a mysterious civilian had approached and tried to sell me a bren-gun carrier. My tendency to fantasy gained immense impetus in my early days in the Army. I am amazed at what I got away with. Suppose my tale of the bren-gun carrier had been reported to Colonel Sunderland, the stiff, wooden-looking CO of this important training regiment? Once, when I saluted him on the barrack-square with a lighted cigarette in my mouth, the heavens fell.

At Topsham Barracks the comical could be found combined with the mysterious. Why were we sometimes ordered to change from one kind of uniform, from battledress to denims, and then without any apparent reason, back again? Sometimes we had to wear denims *over* our battledress; one man, misunderstanding the orders, tried to wear battledress over his denims instead. He was, I think, the only man in my time who got the coveted 'ticket' of discharge ('lucky sod') which was always being discussed with an envy which in most cases was quite insincere. Why was a certain sergeant-major known as 'Grandma'? Once, on some fatigue duty or other connected with the disposal of waste, I found, in a remote part of the barracks, a mysterious hut made out of piles of solidified cardboard, waste paper and flattened salmon tins. An elderly soldier, who looked as though he had been made out of the same materials, lived in it and, it seemed, slept in it. How long had he been living there? Did the Lieutenant Quartermaster of the Regiment, another elderly man who was very good on military songs – my favourite was 'The Quartermaster's Stores', whose plaintive notes still ring through my head from time to time, inducing hopeless nostalgia – did this important and reputedly unscrupulous officer even know that the mysterious hut and its occupant existed?

What did we do when we were not marching about, doing PT under the direction of men known as 'bloodshot wasps' because of their red and yellow striped jerseys and thought, because of their high voices, to be 'queer'; eating disgusting yet welcome meals at times which would have seemed unthinkable to me in 'civvy street', supplemented by buns and bottles of Bass in the Naafi? A scene in our Nissen hut comes to mind. Half a dozen men are sitting round, some on the floor, some on packing cases, shining their boots or buttons or oiling their rifles. From time to time a melancholy, wavering chant arises: 'South of the Border, Down Mexico Way ... Der der der der, der der der der ... South of the Border ...' Suddenly a single voice says in a flat tone: 'Fucking arseholes!' Nobody takes any notice whatever. All know exactly what he means. He is expressing a feeling of disgusted yet cheerful wonder. Why are we here? What are we supposed to be doing? Is it a dream?

For me this life as a gunner, a private soldier in the proper sense, sceptical and ironical, yet doing whatever I was told to do, however absurd, was over all too soon. The British Army was supposed to be a democratic army, in which all, whether they were dukes or dustmen, served initially in the ranks. So (with obvious exceptions) they did. But those who appeared intelligent and 'educated' were very soon plucked from the ranks and formed into a special squad of 'potential officers' (the 'PO Squad'). I was one of these.

Thenceforward life at Topsham Barracks, though still amusing, became less continuously so. We were expected to work harder than the rank-and-file we had left behind, to take training more seriously. Those who did not or could not or would not, soon found themselves back with the rank-and-file again, or, in the case of the intelligent but unsoldierly, were made 'specialists' in signalling or the other primitive electrical skills which were all the Army knew at that time.

I was quite determined not to be returned to the rank-and-file or to be made a 'specialist' (being weak to the point of imbecility in mathematical or engineering skills, I would not have made even a tolerable one, anyhow). What kept me in the 'PO Squad' for all those weeks of training and retraining which were to lead in due course to the interview board at Taunton, the OCTU (or Officer Cadet Training Unit) at Catterick and then to a commission? The mutual support of all the friends I made? An obstinate, even ratlike attitude, learned perhaps, from the rats of Westmorland? Or something about me which convinced the authorities that, however hopelessly unmilitary and even eccentric I seemed, I could not but be, if I was to be anything, an officer?

We were training on real guns now, the once famous 4.5 howitzer 'artillery pieces'; every day of the week except Saturday (because it was inspection day) and Sunday (because it was Sunday) we did gun-drill in teams of six men, changing round for the various duties from the most intelligent duty, that of No. 3, who sighted the gun, to Nos. 5 and 6 who passed the ammunition (wooden shells at this stage) to be shoved into the breach. We also had to be expert at setting up the 'director' on its surveyor's tripod, which gave the guns their angle of fire. We had to dismantle breach-blocks and put them together again as fast as possible. I thought (and probably said) that these beautiful artefacts of shining steel, with their inter-locking sections, pins and bolts, would make delightful Christmas presents. We went out on map-reading expeditions into the beautiful country which lay all round Exeter, sometimes shining all glorious in the snow. I was very good at map-reading, sometimes correcting the errors of the instructor as tactfully as possible. I enjoyed days out on the rifle range, being a reasonably good shot. I was less good, to say the least, at the parts of artillery training which involved elementary mathematics. Was the real reason why I stayed the course that I made remarks which amused our Sergeant Blastfurnace, a huge, red-haired Durham man, with a reputation for ferocity and the heart of a child, by their outrageous pedantry? 'Puts it very nicely, doesn't he?' this redoubtable, much-feared man would say. 'Come on, Gunner Wharton, say something else. I could listen to him all day – but *we haven't got all day*,' he suddenly roared, turning mock-savage in a moment. 'So get fell in! Right Dress!

Number off!' etc. etc. I was for a time, when he would constantly threaten me with relegation to despised 'specialism', a kind of pet or freak. I took full advantage of it.

When, after about six months, I got a statutory week's leave and went back to Westmorland (the journey from Exeter took about twenty-four hours in a blacked-out train and was enlivened by a sailor from Plymouth trying to open a tin of sardines with his teeth and bare hands), I felt a sense of something lacking. It was not that I was not glad to see my wife and child, glad to have a rest from Army life (to sleep between sheets had become an immense pleasure in itself), glad to wander about the familiar lanes and woods and hills. But some meaning had gone out of them. All these things belonged to a phase of life which was now receding into the past beyond recall.

So, putting sadness aside, I was not altogether displeased at getting back to Exeter and its life of organised, dutiful absurdity. It was good to enjoy better physical health than I have ever had before or since; good to have friends to share a whole new world of jokes and technical pleasantries; good to meet women and not think them out of reach.

I think of what may, most improbably, have been one of the longest periods of sustained happiness I ever knew in my life, in a fine week of early summer in 1941. Although the invasion scare was over, perhaps *because* it was over, our battery, including the 'P O Squad', were sent to establish gun positions on the top of some cliffs near Torquay. It was glorious weather; for four days we dug, we fixed up camouflage nets, we ate Army stew out of our mess-tins and drank some Devon cider which we had secreted; and at sundown we went back in our trucks to barracks, singing those melancholy songs. One luminous evening, when the scent of may seemed to pervade the whole world and the evening star had a supernatural brightness, the truck I was in broke down somewhere in Torquay and we stumbled into some 'posh' hotel, all sweaty and dirty as we were in our mud-stained denims. I spoke some German and very soon became an object of suspicion to some officious RA F policeman. Threatened with arrest, I produced my soldier's pass-book, that AB64 in whose convenient back-flap it was the done thing in those days to keep a single French letter, symbol of sophistication. The RAF man seemed mollified, but still suspicious. Perhaps he was right to be so. We got back to barracks at three in the morning, caring nothing that we had to be up again by six.

Soon after that all those who had passed the selection board at Taunton (how much better in every way was that interview, from the first smashing salute I made on entering the room, to the second, even more smashing salute I made when turning on my heel to leave, than the wretched, craven, drunken 'Viva' at Oxford, only five years before!) were made up to Lance-Bombardier, so that before proceeding to OCTU we could learn some of the elementary habits of command. It was the proudest, most improbable title I have ever borne. That evening, after sewing on my single stripe, I entered the bar of The White Lion for an evening's celebratory drinking. But I had been upstaged. An hour before, the news of Rudolf Hess's flight from Germany in search of the Duke of Hamilton had come over the wireless.

How could anyone talk or think of anything else? It was the moment when, after the conquest of the Balkans and Crete, the Nazi Empire in Europe was at its zenith, as yet one long triumph without a single setback. We talked, wallowing in ignorance of what all this might mean. Wisely, no doubt, I kept my own opinions to myself. But I could not see then, and cannot see now, why it would have been more disgraceful for us to make a pact with the Germans in May 1941 than it was for the Russian Communists to make a pact with the Nazis in August 1939. We do not know what the consequences of doing so would have been. But we do know what the consequences of *not* doing so have been. We have only to consider the world as it is in 1984.

I did not go on thinking much about these things at the time. As a Lance-Bombardier I now had to drill new recruits, both in rifle and gun drill. I shouted the commands which not long before had been shouted at me – and sometimes, while thus engaged, I caught the sardonic eye of Sergeant Blastfurnace upon me and heard his encouraging roar: 'That's it, Bom, gi' 'em a good bellow!'

So far the Army had treated me with unexpected kindness. It had also made me physically healthy and driven out my tendency to melancholia, though not my fondness for curious fancies, for which material lay about me in quantities greater than at any time before or since.

The Army, of course, moves (or moved then) in a mysterious way. Because of some error of computation, a 'back-log' of cadets had built up, and I and my fellow temporary acting lance-bombardiers were kept kicking our heels, fulfilling no really useful function, for about two months before we were posted to OCTU. We were a mixed lot indeed: a Cary, belonging to a Somerset farming family who were said to be the most cunning people in England; Harry Rée, a brilliant, energetic, very brave young man, trilingual, part-Jewish, who left suddenly one day to join the Intelligence Corps and later became a hero, much decorated, of the French resistance; an Oxford don; a Lancashire manufacturer; patrician young men who, starting as Gunner Fitzhardinge-Berkeley (a particular butt of Sergeant Blastfurnace) or Gunner Skaife-D'Ingerthorpe, soon found themselves lance-bombardiers, with styles and titles of extravagant fantasy.

But it was not a good time for morale. Something of my old torpor began to come over me; I drank too much (I was still slyly supplementing my income of 7s. 6d. a week by writing occasional pieces for *Punch*, drawing on the fantasies of Army life. One piece, about Sergeant Blastfurnace and RSM 'Grandma', who had asked me to teach him Greek and oil his cricket-bat, was 'brought to their notice', by Harry Rée, I think, and they became puzzled and less friendly).

We were sent on leave quite a lot, and I was able to show off my stripe in Westmorland. On one of these leaves, on a beautiful midsummer morning, we heard the news that the Germans had invaded Russia. Like many people, I thought the German army, undefeated after two years of war, would make short work of the Russian Communists. I was German enough, and, more to the point, anti-Communist enough, to hope so. This may sound outrageous, but the diabolical nature of the Nazi doctrines was not so apparent then as it is now. The Germans, too, had better uniforms and a suggestion of romantic evil which had a certain sinister attraction for people like myself. There is no doubt which side Alexis Saburov, Russian though he was, would have been on in this campaign.

It seemed to me that to have been a German tank commander on that first morning, waiting on the fragrant turf, with the larks singing, for the order to advance into the blue distances of Russia, would have been to experience true military glory, perhaps for the last time in the history of the world. Were not the German armies, as they advanced through White Russia and the Ukraine, welcomed at first as liberators, with flowers and crucifixes? And all this glory, through perverse stupidity, they were to throw away. It does not do to think of these things.

Recalled to Exeter from one of these frequent leaves, I was ordered almost at once to proceed to the Artillery OCTU at Catterick, not a great way from our cottage in Westmorland. So a much more serious phase of life began. Catterick had the reputation of being a 'hard' OCTU, with a higher proportion of men made 'RTU' (returned to unit), as not being 'officer material', than most. I needed all my cunning to survive. But here again some obscure spell seemed to be working. Men who would obviously have made much better officers than I were '

RTU', often to their great resentment. In 1941 the class system was still in being. I did not really belong to any class. But I looked and talked as if I belonged to the officer class. And so I somehow *had* to become an officer, even though I could not really understand the elementary mathematics involved in gunnery and was probably the worst driver who was ever reluctantly passed as fit to hold a driving licence by Bombardier Lewis, my patient young instructor. He was a Welsh-speaker and was therefore so amazed and gratified by my knowledge of the language that he overlooked my inability (never overcome) to start a vehicle on steep hills or bring it to a standstill within five yards of the point desired. I have always found it difficult to do more than one thing at a time and driving a car, like playing a piano, involves this very common ability.

However, even if I was unfit to drive I was capable of studying the working of the internal combustion engine. I found it fascinating. It was no abstract thing, but a complicated toy with, it seemed and seems, a crude, even fanciful and intestinal mode of operation. In the written examination we cadets had to take on this subject, I got a mark of 96 per cent. My diagrams of the gear-box were very beautiful. A month later I could not have told anyone a single thing about it.

The Commandant at Catterick was a pleasant, genial gentleman, Colonel Waller, a landowner with an estate quite near Catterick, over in County Durham. One of his specialities was a short written general knowledge paper which he devised himself. It was evidently designed to test the cadets' fitness for a commission. One of the questions in my own paper was: 'What is the female of a blackcock?' I was the only cadet in my battery who got the answer right (it is, of course, a greyhen). It is possible that I owed my commission to this bit of information, picked up, I think, from a Westmorland gamekeeper.

Soon after this general knowledge test there was a big batch of 'RTUs'. There were some angry looks among the rejected

ones as they packed their kitbags and prepared to leave. There
was a good deal of muttering ('If your face fits, all right') and a
general determination to wring the neck of any greyhens they
came across in future. I believe it was about this time that some
democratic rag, perhaps the *Daily Mirror*, got up an agitation
about people like Colonel Waller ('Are these the men we want
to train our Officers . . .?', 'Britain's Snob Army . . .' and so
on). It may have been no coincidence that the good Colonel
Waller left soon afterwards and was replaced by Colonel Jackson,
a very different kind of man who may not even have known or
cared what a blackcock was, let alone a greyhen. This newcomer
took an instant dislike to me and would, I think, have dearly
loved to 'RTU' me (he once found me reading Virgil, a writer
Colonel Waller had been fond of and had discussed with me).
But by then I had reached the last month of training. I wore
the magic double white tapes on my shoulder-straps which
confirmed my selection for a commission and put me beyond
the reach of the new CO's dull efficiency and egalitarian malice.
My officer's uniform was measured and made and the great
morning came, a fine frosty morning in January 1942 – my
'training' had certainly been a long one – when I and my coevals
dressed up like so many actors for the Passing Out Parade.

After a statutory week's leave, which I spent partly with my wife,
the baby and my parents in their flat in Bradford and partly in
Westmorland (that was a good leave; we were more pleased with
each other than we had been for a long time and my wife, though
perhaps secretly surprised, was proud of my new status), I was
ordered to report to the firing camp at Trawsfynydd in North Wales.
It was strange to travel on the little railway line which crossed the
mountains between Bala and Ffestiniog; to pass, by night, the
enchanted mountain, Arenig, beneath whose crags, only a few years
before, we had tramped the roads and fled from a fierce stallion.
Alone in a first-class carriage, creaking in my new uniform, I

savoured this contrast with pleasure and sadness. What on earth would happen next?

I was surprised to wake next morning in a Nissen hut as a voice said 'Where are we? It looks like the Wild West.' Out of the window I saw the beautiful snow-covered mountains of Ardudwy. It was a sparkling winter day. All that week we drove about the mountain tracks, positioned our guns, checked parallelism, fired off live shells (my first experience of this) then returned to a highly civilised mess where I realised fully the advantages of being an officer. The week was over too soon. It was followed, after the peculiar fashion of the Army, with yet another week's leave.

'He is too passive and lacks initiative.' These negative qualities, which enabled me to float along with the moment, had helped me to become an officer. They also ensured that I did not get a very good first posting. It was to an old yeomanry regiment which had been converted to medium artillery. I had been trained on field artillery – the famous 4.5 howitzers – and knew nothing of medium artillery, except that it was larger and worked in much the same way. This did not seem to matter. The battery I was assigned to was stationed in the southern part of the West Riding. I was billeted in a tiny room at the top of a local magnate's house in a region not unlike the place where I was born, though less hilly, neither town nor country and with collieries and slag-heaps instead of mills. My duties were slight; my fellow officers nondescript and rather boring, except for the commanding officer, a foppish Welshman who always took his corgi dog with him wherever he went. He was not popular; nor was his dog; and I was amused to notice, one day, when we were on some incomprehensible exercise, that when the Colonel's back was turned and he was fiddling pettishly with his binoculars, my sergeant, noted for his sense of humour, shoved the dog into a muddy pond, then rescued it and handed it to its master with a stupendous salute.

I can't say I was kept very busy. I spent a good deal of time walking down the main street of the village where the men of my section were billeted and then walking back again. Nominally I was supposed to see that they were busy at their duties. But they could have got along quite well without me. I spent the rest of my time reading in my billet and in the officers' mess, a very different one from that of Trawsfynydd and with a very different class of officer.

It was not long before I met, at a regimental dance, a tall, fair, spoiled, attractive girl, only daughter of a rich local manufacturer. She supplied an interest in life which might otherwise have been lacking. 'Didn't take you long to get your feet under the table,' said one of my fellow subalterns without much rancour. He had somehow got the idea that I was an actor in civil life. I did not contradict this. But in fact I was more of an actor in military life.

My regiment, which was on vague garrison duties, soon left South Yorkshire and during the next two or three months changed its location several times. This gave us all something to do. As it moved about in a fairly small area in the East Riding and Lincolnshire it was not difficult for my girl friend and myself to snatch occasional meetings, usually in hotels where many of the other guests were probably occupied in much the same way.

I had a remarkable capacity for avoiding air-raids, not by any calculation but by odd coincidence. On the night after I had spent an afternoon in bed with my girl friend in York, it was heavily bombed in one of the 'Baedeker raids' – retaliation for RAF raids on historic German towns and cities – which incidentally reduced many of my old haunts in Exeter to rubble.

It was a time of waiting. My battery was continually going off on inexplicable exercises to places which I would never otherwise have visited: the Yorkshire Wolds; Lincolnshire; the Wash. Certain sights and sounds are vivid: Lincoln Minster, huge at foggy nightfall as we returned in convoy from some exercise or other; a bivouac in straw in a barn down by the Wash at some out of the way place like

Leake or Wrangle, after a day spent firing shells into the mud-flats under a leaden sky; the moaning and whining of the shell fragments; waking on a morning of early summer in my tent in the garden of a magical grange in Tennyson's Lincolnshire, with the birds all singing – a place I have often tried to find again, in vain. And indeed to find it now would mean nothing. I am not the same person who was then bewitched.

It was now May 1942, the mid-point of the war. All this time, while I was going through the motions of training, marching about, returning salutes with my little stick under my arm (British officers still carried them at that time, though they tended to be mislaid and not replaced) or contriving furtive assignations – all this time the most horrific events were taking place in what must be called the real world: men were being blown to bits, burned to death, drowned, buried alive, hideously mutilated; women and children were being dismembered from the air, squashed, eviscerated, plastered like so much bloody jelly on the sides of collapsing buildings. The world was screaming with man-made, God-ordained suffering. What did I and my fellow-soldiers in an England scarcely touched, living, on the whole, better than most civilians, think about all this? The answer is that we scarcely thought about it at all. It was somewhere else; it was the News (at that time almost uniformly bad) on the wireless in the mess, preceded or followed by 'ITMA'; we had been lucky so far (were we even thankful for that?); but our time would no doubt come.

As a rather useless and idle subaltern I tended to be sent on 'courses', in effect a week's leave in some novel or unvisited spot. This could be useful for meeting my girl friend and it was surprising how enterprising we became. A week spent on instruction in 'tropical hygiene' in the park of some big house in the Home Counties comes to mind – the lectures when drowsiness was hard to overcome, the strolls among the shrubbery, the demonstration, which nearly caused a chain-reaction of disasters, of how to make an 'oil and water flashfire' to dispose of rubbish in jungles yet unvisited. I have never to this day had occasion to make one.

I had just learned that I was to be sent on a heavy tractor driving course at Prestatyn when, in the manner of the Army, everything was suddenly changed. I and a fellow-officer were posted to a field artillery regiment which was mobilising to go abroad. So, abandoning plans to get my girl friend from Yorkshire to North Wales, I found myself in Northumberland, with the proud rampant lion badge of a Scottish division on my arm. The regiment I was joining was a very different outfit from the yeomanry. It was efficient and keen and its officers were of a better class, though not, in general, less boring. The CO belonged to a landowning Anglo-Irish family but, mysteriously, had a Swedish title. He was a mild, social man with no fire-eating characteristics.

My battery commander, Major Crick-Balderton, had plenty. He was a small, energetic, fierce-looking man with sharp features, not, I imagine, unlike Montgomery, at that time about to take over the North African campaign. He was full of what he called 'wheezes', and knowing that I was a bookish sort of chap, asked me if I thought it would be a good wheeze to run off a few dozen copies of Kipling's 'If' and have the officers read out the poem to their men every morning on parade. I said I did not think it was a good wheeze. But he went ahead with it all the same. When my turn came to read 'If' to my section I only just managed to get through it without laughing. Several of the men did not manage it and technically I should have put them on a charge. I did not do so, thinking it unfair unless I could put myself on a charge as well.

We were due to embark for an unknown destination in about six weeks' time, and were extremely busy counting and checking our stores. I was first billeted in the regimental headquarters, a fine old house north of Alnwick, not far from Chillingham, where Lord Tankerville kept his herd of white cattle, descended from the wild cattle of ancient times. Later on, my battery was stationed nearer

Alnwick, around a smaller but still acceptable country house which made a pleasant officers' mess; the other two batteries were stationed around other country houses, in which Northumberland abounds. Once again the Army had brought me to a part of England I had never visited before, and a very beautiful one. It was early summer and I welcomed the expeditions we made in the surrounding countryside. I was sent on various errands which involved driving an Army truck. I did not thereby get much better at driving, reversing tactlessly on to a trim lawn at our battery headquarters rather than knock down the stone gateposts with their heraldic gryphons – a difficult choice.

Once I was sent with a party of men all the way to Newcastle to collect some stores or other (we were always collecting stores). The errand, whatever it was, did not take long, so, as we were not due back before nightfall, we occupied ourselves in getting drunk in different hostelries (as an officer I could not drink, let alone get drunk, in the same places as the men). By the time we were due to return we were all drunk, but the men were drunker than I was, particularly the driver. So there was nothing for it but to drive myself. It was probably my greatest military achievement up to that time, particularly as the truck was of a new American type then beginning to arrive in England and had its steering-wheel on the 'wrong' side. Did these men realise what danger they were in? It was lucky they were anaesthetised by drink. As their lingering songs turned to snores I did my duty and, to my own amazement, delivered them safely back to camp, prudently stopping the truck about fifty yards from its proper place, where I should almost certainly have crashed it into a wall.

One day we were all issued with tropical kit. This, I said in the mess, obviously meant we were bound for Iceland. Major Balderton gave a sharp, barking laugh. But I could see he was not amused. He was, in fact, coming to regard me with suspicion. Next day the whole regiment, wearing the new tropical kit, paraded before the

CO. In our pith helmets and knee-length, buttoned-up khaki shorts
we looked ridiculous and knew it. The Colonel looked as ridiculous
as any, though he had had his shorts tailored and his pith helmet,
unlike mine, seemed to be a reasonable fit. He gave us a gentlemanly
pep-talk and dismissed us to our never-ending checking of stores,
with its accompaniment of traditional Army jokes ('piss-pots, rub-
ber, lunatic officers for the use of, six,' etc. etc.).

During these activities I got to know some of the NCOs
rather better than I knew the officers. On the whole they were
much more interesting people anyhow, with greater maturity and
experience of life. So I quite enjoyed being duty officer at nights,
walking the paths among the trees with Sergeant Smith or
Sergeant Budgen and talking about all manner of things, from
marriage to the scarcity of glow-worms (there were a few in the
tall grass, however, and Sergeant Smith, a particularly interesting
and agreeable man, greeted their tiny, intense green lanterns
with as much delight as I did). One day, during a roadside stop
on some exercise or other, Sergeant Smith produced a pocket
chess set and we started a game which was not finished, though
he was getting a slight advantage, when we had to move on.
Later Major Balderton, who had noted this unseemly behaviour,
gave me a good ticking off and after that I was constantly given
the boring duty of pay parade, handing out 7s. 6d. (or whatever
it had become by this time) to long lines of men, each of whom
had to step one pace forward, salute, take the money, salute
again, about turn, take one pace back and retire. Once, to save
time, I arranged to have my hair cut while paying the men.
Major Balderton gave me another ticking off for this early
example of time and motion study.

For a few days we all went to the firing range at Otterburn.
This, in spite of heavy rain, was pure delight. The rolling moors
of Northumberland, stretching unfenced all the way to the Border
and beyond, with their copses and green mosstroopers' tracks,

were then all beautiful open country, not yet blanketed with the huge, horrible parody 'forests' of Sitka spruce which have turned their Border poetry into Canadian prose. We lived in tents (I had a batman, Gunner Runcie, who had the knack of seeing that I was as comfortable as possible. He was, I think, a bigamist. This is beside the point). At the end of the week we officers went to The Redesdale Arms in the village, dined well by wartime standards and got ritually drunk, some of my fellow-officers turning out to be more interesting than they had seemed. I was late on parade for our return journey next morning and, what made things worse, had put on my smart officer's raincoat, with its warm lining, against the cold, wet weather. I was improperly dressed. 'Take that thing off,' said Major Balderton, 'and wear your greatcoat like everybody else.' It was another black mark for my mounting score.

The time of leaving for a destination unknown but guessed at (our tropical kit had not been replaced by arctic fur and skis) was near. I had ten days' embarkation leave. I spent the first few days with my girl friend, staying in the North Yorkshire moors; the rest in Westmorland with my wife and child. We went on foot or by bicycle about the familiar haunts, the lanes, woods, becks and hills for what we knew would be the last time. There was a certain place, on a well-known path by a woodside, where we took our leave of the last vestiges of that life in Westmorland. It was a bright June day with a mild breeze. A bough creaked, over and over again, with what seemed to me then (I have never forgotten it) a musical, elegiac note. Then came the parting at the station, the last sight of my wife and child, the sad settling back in the railway carriage, watching all that had been familiar slide away. It was a scene which must have been going on at that same moment not only in England but in all parts of the warring world. Back in Northumberland there was more checking of stores; a day when our country house headquarters became empty of the soldiery who had briefly occupied it; and then, on a late afternoon of midsummer, green and golden, the last parade.

A corner seat in a compartment of a blacked-out train full of troops and equipment; a journey with many stops throughout the night; occasional distant explosions which I had learned to ignore; then grey morning light revealed what could only be the waterfront of Liverpool and the great buildings I had last seen only eight years before on my solitary foray into Ireland. Now I was not to know solitude for a very long time. I was a subaltern in an artillery regiment bound, as we now knew, for India, a very small part of the Army indeed but carrying, as Major Balderton had told us in one of his shrill pep-talks, great responsibilities. I had no great sense of this, only of being myself, in an extremely strange situation. Unlike my fellow subalterns I was playing a part, a part which had become second nature by now, but a part nonetheless. Passive and lacking initiative, I was carried along in the stream of events.

After a time – I have no idea how long– all military activities, particularly the movement of men and stores, are very confusing – I found I was looking at the waterfront of Liverpool from the deck of a great liner. It was the P & O liner *Orion*, converted to a troopship, but, as I soon found with pleasant surprise, only partially converted. The officers' quarters were positively luxurious. I shared a smallish cabin with three other subalterns, none of them particular friends of mine but possible to get along with (they were a bit put off by the books I had brought with me: Yeats's *Last Poems* and *A Vision*, which I read constantly, believing it to be a key to much that was going on in the world, and Volume One of Spengler's *Decline of the West*, which I had found, as an other rank, fitted neatly into my 'small pack'). But the bunks were comfortable and the washing arrangements satisfactory.

The ship still had civilian stewards. It still had, for the officers, great dining-rooms with separate tables, snowy white tablecloths and gleaming silver. There were five courses for breakfast, including kedgeree and eggs done in any way you chose. In the bars and the great saloon where we spent much of our spare time, stewards were on hand to serve unlimited amounts of pink gin at about 5*d*. a go, as well as most other drinks you could desire. Not finding any very congenial drinking companions among the officers of my own battery, I found some among others of the numerous units – mostly tanks and artillery – on board. I made one faithful friend, a young signals subaltern who seemed to find my continual fantasising about the ship, the people on it and the voyage itself, quite irresistible. We often sat at a table in the centre of one side of the great saloon, immediately underneath the legend, set out in large gilt letters on the wall, 'Fear God and Honour the King', and, as somebody told me later, became known by those nicknames.

The contrast between the officers' comfortable quarters and semi-civilian life and the quarters, if such they could be called, allotted to the other ranks below decks was staggering. As I found – it was part of my duty to descend to these nether regions to see to the welfare of my men, though how I was to do that was not clear to me – they were crowded together like convicts, some sleeping in hammocks, some on 'biscuits' and blankets on the deck itself. It was appallingly hot down there even before the ship began to move; later it became an inferno, stinking of unwashed bodies and in rough weather of vomit. But I heard no complaints, except the habitual, half-jocular grumbling of the British 'khaki beast'. They accepted their lot without question. It seems incredible now that they did not mutiny. But even if they knew the full extent of the contrast between their sweaty hell and the comfort up above – and it is possible that they didn't – I don't think they would have been outraged. They knew their place. I knew my place – for while I was in the Army I had a place, identifiable by uniform and badges of rank, temporary and unlooked for as it was. I was not outraged by the difference, as Harry Rée, the heroic socialist of Topsham

Barracks days, would have been. He would not have tried to organise a mutiny. But he might have organised – as he once did at Exeter – a 'voluntary compulsory' concert of classical music for other ranks in the officers' saloon, which would have been cleared of drinkers for the purpose. He would thus have annoyed everybody for their own good.

The *Orion* stayed at Liverpool for an inexplicable length of time. But eventually she cast anchor and began to move. Through a haze of pink gin I saw the sea. Next morning I looked out of the porthole and saw, instead of Liverpool, unknown Scottish islands with green hills, brown moors, white sands and here and there white crofts. This was the last of home. We headed out into the Atlantic to join a very large convoy bound for South Africa. It was the end of June, but it was something like a month before we reached our destination, taking a circuitous course which brought us almost to the coast of South America to avoid the German U-boats, then at the height of their campaign.

In this convoy the *Orion* had its own allotted and unvarying position, somewhere in the middle, I was glad to note, of several lines of ships great and small. So every morning I woke to see this steady progress through waters at first grey and gloomy-looking, then, as we steamed south-west, turning blue in ever warmer weather. I had several turns on night watch – the only time I was alone – and searched the sky as the familiar constellations dropped away and stars unseen before appeared to my wondering, would-be astronomer's eyes. I saw Canopus, second in brightness only to Sirius in all the sky, and then the great stars of the Southern Cross. What I did not see or even hear of throughout the entire voyage was a single U-boat. Aware that one of these might be lurking about, that at any moment a rending explosion might hole the great ship, I simply did not think about the matter at all.

It was a pleasant voyage. My duties were slight. There was occasional drill and PT. I had got hold of an Urdu textbook

and knowing that I was 'a bit of an intellectual' Major Balderton
set me the task of giving volunteers among our battery lessons
in the language. I worked quite hard at this, keeping two or
three jumps ahead of my pupils, who, of course, had no textbooks.
They learned a bit of the language in a lackadaisical way, all
except one lance-bombardier, a future Communist shop-steward
perhaps, who would resentfully argue with me about points of
grammar and syntax.

One of my other duties was to censor the men's letters home.
Some of them were writing roughly identical letters to several girls
at once; one man, a big good-humoured gunner with every reason
for good humour, as many as five. Another man, a dark gentle-faced
young gunner, just married before embarkation, was writing love-
letters of great tenderness and even beauty to his young wife; in
fact they were so well-written that I was tempted to tell him so. I
had a feeling (though I do not know if it proved so) that he was one
of those fated to be lost and that he would not see his grieving bride
again.

As I could read Welsh I was given most of the Welsh letters of
all units to censor. I noted, with some asperity, that they were not
usually written in very good Welsh; some contained a good deal of
'OK' and 'blydi well'; the Welsh language is short of swear-words,
ferocious as it can be made to sound.

So the time passed: the sun, straight overhead, showed we had
crossed the Equator; it grew hot; we sweated at our PT; the
wretched soldiery below decks sweltered away; there was a falling
off in attendance at my Urdu lessons. We turned eastward. For a
time it grew colder; there was a swell of great waves as I went on
watch one sunset and knew we were rounding the Cape, with
nothing but the Antarctic to the south. On a certain day birds
appeared. Soon we were docked in the port of Durban. Here we
parted company with most of the convoy, which was bound for
Egypt.

For a week we stayed in the Imperial Transit Camp, ten miles or so from the city. We smelt the curious peppery smell of Africa; saw strange flowers and trees; we were allowed to go into Durban on pass, in the afternoons and evenings. Most of the white people of Natal (and at that time we hardly noticed there were any other people, apart from the extortionate Indian taxi-drivers) were friendly enough. Once in an hotel ('the hotel') I saw a group of white people looking at us in a hostile way. They were the dreaded Ossewabrandwag, we were told, the pro-German, anti-British Afrikaaners.

Meeting an attractive and intelligent girl in a night-club called the 'Stardust', of which officers in transit were made temporary members, I arranged to meet her next day on the steps of the General Post Office. To my surprise and some alarm, she turned up, and in an hour or so I had fallen in love with her. Sophie was a small, fair, graceful girl, Scots of Natal, sympathetic and willing. I spent all the rest of my available time with her, much of it in the 'Stardust', a strange South African version of the clubs Constantine had introduced me to in London. We had a hasty parting. I did not want to be posted 'absent without leave', though tempted to risk it. Later on I wrote love-letters to her, but got no answer. There would be other transient subalterns for her in the 'Stardust'. But being seen with this surprising beauty made my stock rise sensationally with my fellow officers when we resumed our voyage. Escaping from the other half of 'Fear God and Honour the King', I was even invited (only think!) to play poker with Old Etonians.

Now, all about us, the Indian Ocean smiled and smiled, exactly as I had imagined it. We saw dolphins, beautiful, iridescent flying fish. Although the Japanese whom we were going to fight were then at the height of their success (there were reports that they were going to invade Ceylon and even had their eyes on Madagascar), we had no cause to fear their submarines. On a day in early August we saw birds again, perhaps the dreaded 'shitehawks' we were told were one of the horrors of India, which, according to the general view, was an utterly horrible country. 'You can smell the fucking place miles out from Bombay,' I was told by ancient quartermasters. In fact, the smell, smoky, fragrant from burning dung and quite different from the smell of Africa, seemed languorous and not unpleasant.

4
Adrift in India

As it happened, we reached Bombay on the very day in August 1942 when the leaders of the Congress party, with Jawaharlal Nehru at their head, were arrested. Small, excited but aimless-looking mobs of brown people dressed, if they were dressed at all, in dirty white, were roaming about, crying 'Quit India' and throwing stones. But, busily transferring ourselves and our stores from ship to train, working at night by arc-lights, we thought little about them, if at all. On an afternoon of great heat our train set off inland. India, brown and green, looking more like an enormous golf-course than anything else I had ever seen before, swirled about us, dusty, inexpressibly alien and strange.

We seemed to spend weeks in the train, waking, sleeping, doing nothing in particular, as it slowly puffed across the middle of India, sometimes stopping, for no apparent reason, among bright-green paddy-fields where skeletal figures stooped, or at a wayside station with its name-board in English and in the thick, overlined Nagri characters I had not yet learned to read, where a few people strolled aimlessly about or slept in the shade. While we waited, a bullock-cart creaked slowly over a level-crossing. In the unfamiliar trees small monkeys chattered and busily flea'd their young, or fought over a scrap of bread flung to them from the train. Sometimes, after going rapidly and purposefully forward for several miles, the train slowed down, stopped, went a few miles backwards, then forwards again.

An American officer on his way to some liaison post in Calcutta, perhaps, hatless in the sun and in long trousers, scornful of the lectures we had had from medical officers warning us to wear our pith helmets ('Bombay bowlers') or risk dropping dead within minutes, forced me to play liar dice with him for several days on end. It is a game I have disliked ever since. We crossed great rivers, shrunk to small channels among sand and boulders, on which brown, slender women, rousing a faint impulse in men long celibate, were bashing their meagre, coloured cloths. We passed through great stretches of open grassland with groves of broad-leaved sâl trees; denser jungles, isolated rocky hills of fantastic shape, some with what looked like ruined forts or temples on their summits, and, further off, higher ranges fading into blue distance. At night small fires broke out in mud villages; groups of people, chattering, gesticulating and spitting the crimson juice of betel nut, came together, dispersed, reassembled, sat down, fell asleep. There seemed no reason why this journey should ever end.

It ended, at last, at the smallish town of Ranchi in the Province of Bihar, an impoverished, densely forested part of India which had many Army training camps. In one of these, a few miles out of the town, we found ourselves, after a period of indescribable confusion, installed in tents in an open part of the forest. I write 'found ourselves' because I have no recollection, myself, of doing anything to bring this about. At one moment I was getting out of the familiar train into glaring heat which, as I knew it would from my reading, 'hit me like a blow': I was aware of passing in a truck, with others, through a dusty street crowded with shouting people (one, bolder than the rest, may have shouted 'Quit India!' and received from some sardonic NCO the unintelligible reply, 'With pleasure, mate!'); of seeing incomprehensible shops full of broken objects, jars, ancient gramophones, piles of fly-infested sweetmeats, bottles of virulent green and purple mineral water, an enormous pair of false teeth painted on a board, signs – 'Ayurvedic medicine, egg and chips, lemonade, spectacles, food'; and finally of sitting in my officer's tent, one of a long row, which was just big enough to contain my folding bed (with mosquito net) and my tin trunk for sitting on. The legs of the bed were built up on bricks standing in tins of shallow water, to prevent white ants from eating the bed itself. In their search for food and other necessities these ants, which operate in darkness, were swiftly constructing raised tunnels in the earth-floor of the tent; observing them provided something to do until the next event occurred.

At nightfall, dutifully putting on my pith helmet, I walked to the larger mess-tent, where Major Balderton never failed to tell me I looked just like a character from 'one of Noël Coward's plays about life out east' (which were those?). Mad on salutes, he rebuked me several times for failing to salute him. Once, having to wait on him when he was taking a bath in his tent, I saluted so vigorously that part of the tent collapsed. It is fair to say that instead of being angry he gave a shrill, mad cackle. 'Wait for the rains!' he shouted.

Soon after we arrived in this camp the rains, eagerly awaited in the outrageous heat, suddenly broke one afternoon when I was sitting in my tent, wondering, as so often, what on earth I was supposed to be doing. The rain began to come down in what seemed a solid mass. A shrill scream of joy told me that Major Balderton had rushed out of his tent in his underpants, which he had often told us was the custom when the rains arrived. We soon had more serious things to attend to, digging channels round our tents to prevent the water washing them away. Steam rose from the ground with a strange, rich smell. It was as though we were inhaling curry. Thunder rumbled about in a splendid way and as night fell the sky was lit by glorious violet lightning. I have always enjoyed thunderstorms. This was a storm of the highest quality.

The same performance went on for several days, the rain descending punctually at exactly the same time in the afternoon, then easing off for a display of distant lightning. The temperature fell to a bearable 95 degrees or so at midday, making it possible to think of doing some 'training'. The surrounding area west of Ranchi, beautiful hilly jungle and open woodland, was very suitable for this. The inhabitants were aboriginals, dark, graceful, shy people dressed in nothing but small loincloths and beads, with scarlet flowers of 'flame of the forest' in their hair. Sometimes by day, as I was saluting Major Balderton or checking some stores, I would be aware that one of these grave, quiet people, carrying a bow and a few arrows, was passing softly over the grass a short way off among the trees. Once, in evening twilight, I saw one raise his bow as if in salute, though neither to Major Balderton nor myself but to the crescent moon.

Quiet and furtive as they went about their business during the day, these people seemed to spend their nights in endless festival, to the sound of drums, flutes and wild singing. Their villages or settlements were, of course, strictly out of bounds. Many soldiers (and even officers) said they envied this carefree way of living, which certainly seemed to me both happier and better than ours. But Major Balderton, a teetotaller and lifelong bachelor (he once described, at breakfast, in apparent innocence, a 'curious dream I had about being in an absolute sea of naked women'), warned us against the potent 'jungle juice', a kind of rice beer, which the natives drank at their orgiastic festivals. It was said that one man, not in my battery, had been severely disciplined for trying to gatecrash, and another, unable to resist following one of their undoubtedly lissom young women into the jungle, had disappeared altogether.

One by one, as gleefully predicted by Major Balderton, we succumbed to dysentery, which ruled out all activities except excretion and left the sufferer weak, limp and careless whether he lived or died. None died, but several had a few days in hospital in Ranchi, to be dosed with caolin – a not unpleasant spell off duty. I was one of them. Major Balderton, on a routine inspection of the slit trenches, then in constant use, discovered that one sufferer in extremis, finding no other material to wipe his bum, had used pieces of a large-scale ordnance map of the district. The culprit was, of course, myself. This amused him hugely.

Ranchi itself, for all its initial strangeness, seemed a dull little town. It had a small club, however. All officers were made honorary members, and we were generally allowed to go there for the Saturday evening dance. There was only one attractive girl among the Europeans who went there, the dark-haired daughter of a local tea-planter. I met her again, by chance, when after quite a short time, in the curious manner of the Army, I was given a fortnight's leave in the nearest hill-station, Darjeeling.

The long journey there by train and funicular was strange and dreamlike. I woke one morning to find the train had stopped (as usual, for no particular reason) on a great dusty plain. Small boys stood by the line holding bantams' eggs in thin brown palms. 'Boil egg, sahib! Boil egg!' I bought one or two, though advised not to eat them, and, being now immunised against dysentery, took no harm either from them or from the small earthenware pipkins of tea and horribly sweet and sticky buns older vendors were offering. Suddenly I noticed, to the north, a high bank of cloud lying over wooded hills. But it was no cloud. It was the range of the Himalaya.

I had never seen high mountains before. The effect was stupendous, and later, when we reached Darjeeling, I could hardly take my eyes off the great mountain Kanchenjunga all the time I was there. As was the custom, I toiled up Tiger Hill, breathless in the rarefied air, and saw, a hundred miles away, the peak of Everest, with its eternal plume of snow blown by the wind out of Tibet. It was, of course, the most wonderful thing I had seen since the total eclipse of the sun in 1927 – we had been given a school holiday to see that – could it possibly have been only fifteen years before? Did I feel, when gazing at Kanchenjunga and Everest, the numinous sensation of my youth?

I doubt it. I believe that even then – I was only twenty-nine – I was beginning to feel its loss, that indescribable 'feel of not to feel it' which Keats could do no more than state, though Coleridge, in his ode 'Dejection', comes closer to putting it into words. The tea-planter's daughter was fond of poetry and I used to read it to her. Once Major Balderton saw us in a rickshaw together, moving down a tree-lined road in the cantonment of Ranchi. 'I see you're a bit of a poodle-faker, Wharton,' he said later in the mess, with his mad, screaming laugh. It was another black mark.

His opportunity to get rid of me came fairly soon. With some other young officers I was asked to a party at the tea-planter's bungalow and, drinking too much, fell asleep in one of the bedrooms, to wake in the morning much bitten by mosquitoes and technically absent without leave. Back at the camp I was relieved of my revolver, put under arrest and escorted by two fellow-officers to receive a reprimand and seven days' confinement to camp. A little later came a request from Corps HQ, under whose command, though a British regiment, we came, for an intelligence officer. I was supposed to be intelligent, was certainly a bit of a nuisance, and so, by no means unwilling, was seconded. Major Balderton's farewell was surprisingly cordial and accompanied by an exceptionally fine mad cackle. The CO seemed genuinely sorry to lose me. Always gentlemanly and mild, he wished me the best of luck.

Corps HQ was in a neighbouring rajah's palace, with marble floors and bathrooms, all marble and gold, of remarkable vulgarity. It was good to sleep under a roof and to take a hand in marking up the maps in the War Room, where they were inspected by the Corps Commander, General Slim, himself. Slim, who though perfectly English, looked like a caricature of a good kind of Australian, was very different from any senior officer I had come across before. He was both intelligent and amiable. He inspired respect, even devotion, and later on, of course, was to prove himself most worthy of them.

I particularly liked marking up the map of the Eastern Front according to the daily reports. The Germans had reached the Caucasus. Did I secretly wish them to advance further? Did I even stick a swastika-flagged pin in Astrakhan on the Caspian Sea, advancing the German Army to a point it never in fact reached? If so, nobody noticed.

There were congenial officers among my fellows in GS(I). One of these, Dick Stovy from Doncaster, shared my liking for fantasy and was to become a lifelong friend, turning up at odd moments during my wartime service both on duty and on leave, and always making life more agreeable. With his co-operation I could make the rather pompous and disagreeable head of our intelligence section, Major Caird-Smith, into an amazing figure of fun.

Our headquarters went out on numerous field exercises into the beautiful hills and jungles of Bihar. These were most enjoyable. At least they seem so now, when seen through the wrong end of a telescope, jewel-bright and with all discomfort smoothed away. Certain scenes remain vivid in memory. I am trying to shave in the wing-mirror of a truck at dawn, while a shimmering mist of delicate pink, green and amethyst rises from the ground as the sun comes up, quickly strengthening and dispersing those veils of dreamlike beauty. I am in the back of a truck bumping along dirt roads that connect remote villages, covered from head to foot in the choking red dust of our progress and rejoicing in the prospect of a good soaking in a canvas bath prepared by a willing bearer.

I am sitting by myself on a boulder in the jungle, not far from a small village where the smell of wood-smoke is strong and fragrant and women can be seen rolling out chapattis on flat stones with their feet or making cakes of buffalo-dung for fuel. There is a sudden trumpeting and swishing noise on the jungle track and there, only a few yards from me is an elephant, no zoo-bound beast but a genuine working elephant with a great load of logs on his back and his master by his side, urging him on with unearthly cries. I am so surprised that I stand up, with an absurd impulse to salute this wonder. The Indian laughs, showing red, betel-stained gap-teeth in a fine, friendly smile. Does the sahib seem as strange to him as the elephant does to me?

Strangest of all, I am lying on my canvas bed, looking at the big clear stars overhead through the meshes of the mosquito net secured for convenience to the tailboard of my truck, and listening, without fear, to the incessant slithering and whispering of countless snakes moving about among the coarse grass and large pink and blue flowers which grow everywhere in the sandy ground.

These were long, copper-coloured snakes, quite harmless. There was another kind of snake, however, which I had already heard a lot about when I was with the regiment. This was the banded krait, which looked like a short length of string on a dusty road. Its venom, according to the excitable Major Balderton, would 'have you whirling round like a catherine wheel and dead in six minutes' – or was it six seconds? The only thing to do, if you were bitten by one of these killers, was to cut out the affected part with a razor-blade. Major Balderton accordingly issued razor-blades to 'all personnel'. According to rumour, one man, thinking he had been bitten by a krait, immediately cut his finger off, only to find later on that what had bitten him was not a krait at all but some relatively harmless reptile. This was generally thought a great joke, though Major Balderton, mindful of his status and authority, refrained from the screaming laugh he must have felt welling up inside him.

After a time I was selected for a course at the Army Intelligence School at Karachi. This meant a three-day journey by train all the way from Asansol on the main line, a centre of the strange Bihar coalfield, worked by sad, tamed aboriginals from the forests, tricked or forced into exchanging their bows and arrows and flowers and all-night parties for money-wages, their graceful nakedness for horrible little khaki shorts. We saw Benares and the great Gangetic Plain, the Indus, the Thar Desert – too many wonders to take in on one journey without suffering visual surfeit and mental indigestion.

The weather was now perfect. In the winter of Northern India, every day between November and February is like a hot English summer day and the nights are cool enough for fires. On a certain pre-determined day in January it rains a little. It is also supposed to rain a little, for reasons acceptable to Christians, on Christmas Day by way of celebration. I am not certain that this is true.

I did not care for Karachi. Even its European Club, though palatial compared with that of Ranchi, seemed rather boring. So, on the whole, did the Intelligence School, in spite of its Commandant, an Ulsterman who, most unsuitably, would shout 'Hi!' as he appeared at his lecturer's desk in the morning, the assembled officers being required to answer 'Ho!' He was like an eccentric schoolmaster dressed in uniform, and many officers laboured hard to perfect their imitations of his voice and stiff, pedantic manner. It would not have been surprising if, at the end of the course, we had all been tested for taking him off accurately and awarded marks accordingly.

This was the time of Stalingrad, of Alamein, of the turning-point of the war, when the defeat of Germany, and consequently the defeat of Japan, was already a foregone conclusion. But most of the exercises we did on the Intelligence course, both in the lecture-room and 'in the field', were still based on the assumption that the Germans would break through the Caucasus, occupy the Middle East and Persia and then try to invade India. Some of the more enjoyable parts of the course were simulated intelligence exercises based on this already far-fetched hypothesis. There was a good 'scenario' or charade in which the German invasion of the Indus Valley was supported by a Muslim uprising and a re-run of the

Indian Mutiny. I was responsible for the role of the Pir Pagaro or some other specimen of those fanatical religious leaders who were always about at that time, rallying ferocious tribesmen, disappearing and re-appearing in a bewildering way, always 'with a price on their heads' and described as 'a thorn in the side of the British Raj'. I invented the Thargs, a fanatical sect who lived in caves in the Sind Desert but were in wireless (or perhaps telepathic) communication with the German High Command. As the first panzers appeared on our side of the Khyber they were ready to 'rise as one man', sacking the bazaars, wrecking trains and sniping from mosques at the British and those Indians who remained loyal to us. As these Thargs had red or even blond hair and blue eyes (they were, of course, direct descendants of Alexander's soldiers) the Germans regarded them as Aryans and Dr Rosenberg, the Nazi racial theoretician, had suggested to Hitler that a Greater Thargia, under German protection, should be set up in most of what is now called Pakistan – an entity not all that much more absurd. I became so enthusiastic about these imaginary Thargs that I was ordered to abolish them.

We also went out on exercises. One of these, which involved wading through foul-smelling mangrove swamps on the Indus Delta, was particularly nasty and dangerous. One officer, who could not swim, was, I think, actually drowned. My own request for a taxi to take me back to dry land and beat the steadily rising tide which was flooding these muddy, noisome creeks, was ill-taken by the directing staff. On another exercise in the Sind Desert, which at least had a definite purpose, map-reading, I found myself separated from the rest by being the only man to read the map correctly. Alone in this barren country, which yet seemed able to support a few goats (since there was no vegetation, what on earth did they feed on?) I sat down on a stony hillside, wondering, as so often, what I was doing here in this improbable place. The winter sun shone in a perfectly blue sky, enough to warm me most pleasantly but not to burn or turn me much browner than I already was; I looked about me into this stony nothingness and felt a surge of that 'oceanic' feeling of inexplicable happiness which even at twenty-nine, as I have said, I was beginning to fear was lost for ever. I felt I might just as well stay where I was, letting this feeling flood over me and through me, as go anywhere else or do anything else. I had an absurd feeling that 'Aunt' might appear. But when some of my fellow intelligence students appeared instead, fiddling with their maps and compasses, I joined them just the same.

There was much that was absurd about the course. It is not really very difficult to be an Intelligence Officer, unless you are concerned with coding, cryptography and all those techniques which in other theatres of war were already beginning to have decisive importance. But we in India and on the borders of Burma were, as the English newspapers put it, 'the Forgotten Front'. As the German offensive into India never materialised, it was to remain forgotten for some time.

One day the Commandant, after going through his 'Hi!' and 'Ho!' procedure, announced that we were going to have a lecture on some of the main races of India – Sikhs, Mahrattas, Punjabi 'Mussulmen', Bengalis and so on. Specimens of various races, dressed in appropriate costume, were paraded before us as in a 'mannequin parade' while an officer pointed out their characteristics with his swagger stick – the last time, I think, I saw this profoundly undemocratic artefact actually used (I had long ago lost mine). As the assorted Indians, smiling in an obliging way, paraded before us, there were some ribald comments from my companions. But only the specimen Sikh looked at all angry. It was as well he had no sword with him.

On the whole it would be true to say that except for those in the Indian Army, who came into personal contact with Indian troops, mostly of the favoured 'martial races', some of whom were now being commissioned, most English (or British) people in India regarded Indians as patently inferior and even ridiculous. When I was with my regiment Major Balderton had ticked me off for speaking Urdu with an authentic accent (though without any real 'gift for languages' I am exceptionally good at mimicking accents). As Major Balderton explained, it was simply not done to speak any Indian language unless with an English accent, preferably that of Camberley.

English women, as is well known, were more habitually rude to Indians than English men. But it was easy to get into the habit of treating them with disdain, of shouting at them for their inefficiency, procrastination, vagueness, weakness in spatial relations or sense of time. Most people found that characteristic oblique nod of the head, which seems to indicate 'yes' and 'no' at the same time, particularly infuriating. I found it delightful and convenient for expressing various shades of unmeaning. I soon found myself, now there was no Major Balderton about to tick me off, using this gesture myself. I still do. I also occasionally use that curious spiral upward movement of the hand and wrist – so attractive in the narrow-boned Indian – which, especially in conjunction with the oblique nod, expresses the complex ambiguity which is said to lie in the very soul of India.

The Intelligence course finished (I had learned a lot without being aware of it), we returned to our units – in my case, the 15th Indian Corps in its rajah's palace in Bihar. It was, as it happened, on the point of moving forward towards the frontier of Burma, where our troops confronted the Japanese in small concentrations in mountainous, jungle country inhabited by non-Indian aboriginal tribesmen such as the Karens and the Nagas.

Nothing much was happening on this 'Forgotten Front' except for a little desultory shelling and patrolling. It was the spring of 1943 and the Japanese, already beginning to be pushed back from the extreme limits of their 'Greater East Asia Co-prosperity Sphere', had no time to spare for their Indian Front. As an intelligence officer I worked on information concerning the Indian National Army which Subhas Chandra Bose, the 'Bengali Fascist', a remarkable and, as it was to turn out, tragic figure, was recruiting from Indian prisoners of war taken in Malaya, Singapore and Burma, and preparing for an eventual invasion of India. I also studied the Japanese-occupied railway system in South-East Asia, with particular attention to making lists of locomotives. But my most interesting work, on the whole, was a study of the private lives of important Japanese generals. Information on this, as on other subjects which concerned military intelligence, was graded in degrees of reliability ranging from 'A' – 'information from very reliable sources' – to 'G' – 'bazaar rumours'. I have since found this system of classification valuable in civilian life. As for the Japanese generals, they did not seem a very exciting lot. Perhaps there was simply not enough information about them. So I invented one – let us call him General Yamaha Mitsutachi – a one-eyed man in his late forties who had spent some of his early years in Bradford, learning the textile trade, whose inmost secrets, needless to say, he discovered in typical Japanese fashion, at once sending them back to Japan for imitation. He had also discovered the secret formulae for Doncaster Butterscotch, Pontefract Cakes, Harrogate Toffee, parkin and Yorkshire pudding and thought up the brilliant idea of building factories in Japan to manufacture these articles, calling the associated workers' estates 'Doncaster', 'Pontefract', 'Harrogate' and so on, so that 'Made in Pontefract' would be a legitimate description of the contents of green-lettered tins which yet had something odd and obscurely Japanese about them.

While in Bradford Mitsutachi had been insulted by Willy Gaunt (a legendary Bradford magnate notorious for his meanness who, though a millionaire, still lodged with his mother for a small weekly rent) in the 'French Restaurant' of the Midland Hotel, where he was entertaining Gaunt to a sumptuous luncheon. He returned to

Japan with the words 'little yellow monkey' festering in his soul and with a burning lust for vengeance. Joining the army, he soon rose to general rank, mystifying his fellow-officers by shouting, in the English he had learned in Yorkshire, 'Bah Gum, I'll get my own back if it's the last thing I do' in a ferocious way and poring over Japanese military maps of the West Riding in which such places as 'Frizinghall', 'Cleckheaton' and 'Gomersal' were ringed with angry scarlet, prime targets for his revenge.

For a few weeks or months I passed my time in such harmless pursuits, enjoying the open air life and the beauties of the jungle until I was recalled and attached to the newly formed Indian Army Public Relations Directorate, which had been invented, elevated into a Department of the General Staff and rapidly expanded into an 'empire' by a remarkable, energetic, red-haired Scot, Brigadier Ivor Jehu. Its officers included, besides myself, some remarkable drop-outs and eccentrics who gave me a lot of material for a fantastic novel which, though I made copious notes, never got written.

One of the main characters was an officer who, while on a motiveless tour of Southern India, got so drunk that he fell out of a train in a remote jungle and was picked up by some kindly aboriginals who nursed him back to health with magical herbs. In return he had nothing to offer except some handouts issued by the Directorate about new types of light tank operated by paraffin which, it was hoped, would strike terror into the Japanese. Delighted, these kindly people tore them into small pieces and sowed them in one of the fields they roughly hacked out of the forest (they used what is called 'the slash and burn' type of cultivation). Soon a miraculous kind of giant maize sprang up. The aboriginals, regarding Captain Snoddie as a minor deity, implored him to stay with them for ever.

This he was glad to do. But on an evil day, tiring of the rice beer which was their only form of intoxicant – he had to drink it in such prodigious quantities even to approach his normal alcoholic intake that he was in danger of becoming dropsical and immobile – he set off for the nearest town, many miles away, in the hope of getting a bottle of whisky. There he fell in with a treacherous ayurvedic dentist, who detained him with flattery and atrocious home-distilled spirit, took his money off him and eventually handed him over to the local magistrate, the hunchbacked Dr Sen, who informed the military. Taken back to Delhi under escort, he was given such a terrible dressing down by Brigadier Jehu himself that he burst into tears and was at once promoted major on compassionate grounds. Another character . . . but enough of these fantasies . . .

The function of the Directorate was supposed to be 'liaison' with the Indian Press, both English and vernacular, and the incessant feeding of Indian journalists with material presenting our forces in a favourable light. It also arranged visits by Indian journalists and public men to Army, Navy and Air Force units and formations and dealt with parties of visitors and 'VIPs' from England, observers from allied and neutral countries and other such matters. It also had other, less publicised functions. When I joined it I did not cease to be an intelligence officer.

Although I am very cowardly by nature I do not think this move, which placed me many hundreds of miles further away from the Japanese, was deliberately contrived by me for that reason. It was one of those chances by which, as I have mentioned before, I found myself, for instance, leaving a particular place just before it was heavily bombed. Nor was my subsequent life in the Army entirely without danger, physical and mental. What my new role did involve (and in this I was greatly privileged) was the opportunity to travel, often entirely alone, to almost all parts of India during the next three years, and to meet more Indians than was at all usual for a British officer.

My first posting was to Agra, headquarters of Central Command, to which I was attached. There, in the spacious cantonment, I was allotted a billet appropriate to my new rank of Captain, a small apartment in a row of brick huts along one side of the maidan, a large square open space recalling part of the Stray at Harrogate rather than anything else. It was, however, mid-June, in the very hot season, with shade temperatures reaching 120 degrees, dust storms, prickly heat, dhobi's itch (an unpleasant eczema of the crotch which the good medical Captain da Cruz treated with the well-known Army cure-all, gentian violet) and, during hours of duty, a condition of lassitude which made it difficult to do anything much except sit at a table in my office hut sifting through papers on every conceivable subject. A punkah waved backwards and forwards overhead, operated by a string held in the strong big toe of an elderly Indian (aged about thirty, I suppose) who sprawled outside on the verandah. In addition, two younger Indians occupied themselves all day in throwing buckets of cold water over the wicker screens, called *khus khus tatti*, which leaned against the outer walls.

What emerges from this haze of lassitude? Now that the German threat to invade India, if it had ever really existed, had receded, probably for ever, now that Mussolini had fallen and the Italians, or most of them, had surrendered (many Italian prisoners were beginning to arrive in India), HQ Central Command at Agra was just about as far as it was possible to get in the Northern Hemisphere, apart from Siberia and North America, from the conflict which every day and night was killing and maiming thousands of people, tearing historic buildings apart and filling the world with grief and hatred. The fact is that we at Agra thought very little about these things. What I was seeing there was a rather obscure corner of the British Raj still in being. The malis still tended the fine lawns and brilliant flower-beds of official bungalows. At night the chowkidar, or night-watchman, still went his rounds, coughing horribly at intervals and feebly tapping his stave on the ground. The dhobi plied his trade. The darzi, or tailor, still sat cross-legged at the door of his shop, obsequiously taking orders for bush-shirts or pyjamas of heavy Indian silk, promising to have them ready without fail within a week and still promising the same after a week, two weeks, three weeks.

The memsahibs, whether they were officers' wives, in which case many of their husbands were away in Africa or Italy or on the fringes of Burma, or the wives of officials of the Indian Civil Service, in which case their husbands were with them when they were not on tour, lived very much in the old style. They gave dinner parties as they had always given them. The port circulated in the proper manner when the ladies retired and the men were left to talk about whatever they had always talked about: promotion, demotion, the impossibility of Indians being able to rule themselves ('give them independence and within a week there won't be a rupee or a virgin between Peshawar and Delhi'). As I was thought to be quite amusing, I was occasionally asked to these dinner parties. Once, when I had had a good deal to drink, no very uncommon thing, I said, à propos of the Russian campaign, that the Russian Communists were not really our allies and that we should not be helping them in any way, since it was better that the Germans should weaken their odious regime and if possible destroy it. There was a bit of silence at this. A Major Atherstone-Smith, rising from his place and going scarlet in the face, said I ought to be court-martialled. I heard nothing further, but noticed his face bulging slightly whenever I came across him afterwards. I wonder whether he still believed in our gallant Communist allies ten or even five years later?

The monsoon, my second in India, broke soon after this, cooling things down a bit to the great relief of all, and once again rain came down not only by the bucketful but at least once in the form of large jagged lumps of ice which probably killed a few Indians. Indians, as everybody knew, could be killed very easily, which was one reason, Major Balderton had often mentioned with his mad cackle, why you had to avoid striking servants, however maddened you might be by their dim-witted incompetence.

At about the beginning of September I took a period of furlough in Simla, the nearest sizeable hill-station. In peacetime the Government of India moved up there en masse in the hot weather. In wartime they stayed in Delhi, but most of their wives and daughters still went to the hills. As young or youngish officers came and went, the more personable of these ladies found themselves greatly in demand and able to pick and choose. After a few days I 'found myself' having an affaire with Margaret, the pretty, fair-haired, blue-eyed wife of an ICS official. She was not, perhaps, the most stunningly beautiful or lucidly intelligent of the European women in Simla, but she was not without admirers. I was soon in love, and so, she told me, was she. I was the more innocent of the two. But at least she made me feel as happy and contented during that leave in Simla as it was in my nature to be.

We met in the mornings at the Green Room Club, part of the Simla Amateur Dramatic Society which at that time was rehearsing *Young Woodley*. We walked about the Mall or among the forest paths on the steep slopes of the spur of the Himalaya on which Simla is built. A Scotch mist, the mountain equivalent of the monsoon, wavered and floated among the pines and strange-looking, rambling bungalows. At certain points, when the mist parted, you could look down beyond the precipices to where, thousands of feet below, the great plains burned in the heat.

Quite by chance, while I was in Simla, I ran into Richard Storry, who had helped me to make Dickensian grotesques out of some of our seniors at Ranchi. He was studying at the Army School of Japanese studies in Simla, and so absorbed had he become with Japanese matters that already his square, reddish, very English face was beginning to acquire a Japanese look. He asked me to dinner at the School, where there was an interesting assortment of officers. One was a man who later on became a best-selling novelist. Another was a huge, moustachioed, bearlike White Russian, born at Mukden in Manchuria. He bent a few iron bars for our amusement (he claimed to have been a strong man in a Korean-owned circus), then bellowed songs in Russian and other languages. We played several traditional mess-games, such as climbing round the walls without touching the floor and billiard fives, a painful, taxing game which involves batting billiard balls about with your bare palms, until we were too drunk to continue.

When the end of my leave came soon afterwards Margaret and I took sad leave of each other, promising to write continually and meet again at the first possible opportunity. Delhi, after all, was only about 150 miles from Agra, quite near in Indian terms. We met only once again, about two years later, and could think of nothing whatever to say to each other. But in the meantime, at odd times and places, I met several officers who had met her on their periods of leave. What we all shared had become, sadly, an unspoken joke.

My fellow staff officers at Agra were a mixed lot. Some were remarkable drop-outs, regular officers like the nominal head of my own department, Lieutenant-Colonel Huzzifreak, a man wizened and prematurely old from service in India. He had been with the 'Piffers' or the 'Paffers' or some such regiment on the North-West Frontier. His main purpose in life was to do as little as possible, which at moments of highest achievement meant absolutely nothing. But he was friendly and amiable enough, his main cross being the third officer in our department, an Indian who was both eager to please and resentful of us two Europeans. When thwarted in any way, such as having his suggestion of going on a tour which would include his native city of Nagpur turned down, he went grey in the face with frustration and anger. But Colonel Huzzifreak dealt with him most effectively by his favourite method of doing and saying absolutely nothing.

Perhaps the most remarkable of my fellow staff officers was Major Charles Rankin, a very good-looking man of upper-class background, not more than two or three years older than myself. He was delightfully urbane and amusing and never at a loss. He was exactly the sort of person I have always (well, sometimes) wanted to be. What his real function in the Headquarters was I never knew – it may have been as ambiguous as my own – but his style and title was General Staff Officer Grade II (Chemical Warfare). Since there was not the remotest chance that chemical weapons would be used in the area of Central Command this meant that he appeared – whatever the real truth of the matter – to have absolutely nothing whatever to do. A good deal of paper came to him daily from GHQ in New Delhi. A lot of it was about defence against mustard gas, phosgene and other substances used on the Western Front in the First World War, or about the use of bleach, brown paper and other things I had last heard of at Topsham Barracks in Exeter. He threw away most of this paper but kept a single large blue file marked 'Most Secret' (the vulgar, ungrammatical, objectionable American 'Top Secret' had not yet been introduced, and was perhaps never to be used in Central Command, that castle of indolence where only rumours penetrated from the tiresome, noisy outer world).

Major Rankin, whose social contacts were obviously on a higher level and often took him away 'on tour', did not attend the Saturday evening dances at the Agra Club, a commodious and agreeable building in one corner of the maidan which for certain purposes also functioned as an officers' mess. Here was a bar, a billiard-room, a dining-room, a small, variegated library which contained, as well as the works of Maud Diver, many of the novels of William Gerhardi, such as his best one, *My Wife's the Least of It*, which I read several times, and a ballroom. It had pleasant gardens, a capacious verandah and terraces where, now that the weather was turning into the wonderful North Indian winter, it was pleasant to sit drinking glass after delicious glass of fresh lime juice, gin and soda.

At the dances a small string orchestra of Indian musicians played such numbers as 'As Time Goes By', 'That Lovely Week-end' and even, by request, 'Begin the Beguine', 'Sand in My Shoes' and 'Stormy Weather' (my own favourites, heavy with nostalgia no more than four years old) in an odd, unreal style. Were these musicians more at home playing authentic Indian music? I never found out and in my early days in Agra I scarcely knew this music existed. I had heard only the debased film music played on raucous gramophones in the bazaar.

The Saturday night dances were mainly an occasion for getting drunk, playing billiards or both. But they also offered an opportunity to meet European ladies who were not, I think, socially of the best class, that is, the class of those who gave dinner parties, cocktail parties and, on occasion, dances of their own. At one of these dances in the Club I met a woman whose husband was said to be a prisoner of war. I had been told, I think by the Station Staff Officer, a man of homosexual temperament, that she had a bad reputation and should be avoided. He even told me he had thought of having her expelled from the cantonment. But in fact he never carried out this threat because he was shortly afterwards required to leave himself.

Harriet was a very small, gamine woman of about thirty, not particularly good-looking but most attractive because of her vivacity, intelligence and the pale reddish hair which is found only among Scotswomen and goes with that white, slightly metallic, freckled skin which for me has always transmitted a sexual current of very high voltage.

We got into conversation, laughed, drank (she turned out to be one of those women who can drink most men under the table) and danced or pretended to dance (I have never been able to dance, but on a small, crowded dance-floor could go through the required motions), under the reproving eyes of several of the officers' ladies who, perhaps for reasons of their own, may have shared the Station Staff Officer's opinion. We slipped away from the Club, crossed the dark maidan to the small bungalow where she lived. I had seldom, if ever, enjoyed such pleasures. I left by climbing through the window in the early hours of the morning, almost bumping into Major Atherstone-Smith whose billet was in a nearby bungalow and whom I had noticed earlier on playing billiards and getting ritually drunk. We did not speak, but I could see he had registered another item to add to my anti-Soviet remarks.

I saw him again next day at the Club where, after sleeping off the various exertions of the night before, it was customary to drink an enormous amount of gin, followed by a huge Sunday lunch of curry, followed by another spell of sleep. Forgetting or only half-remembering Margaret of Simla, I was now in love with Harriet as well. She was quicker, more amusing, better able to share my fantasies and jokes about the denizens of Central Command. She could drink like a man, liked music; and she was not respectable. That was the first of many nights, either in Harriet's room or in my billet, where my quiet Hindu bearer, sleeping on his charpoy or string-bed just outside the back door, must have heard those lovers' gasps and moans, but gave no sign next morning.

What was I doing when I was not making love, drinking, talking nonsense or shuffling papers in an Army hut? 'Staff work' in Central Command consisted mainly in distributing memoranda, the chief amusement in that being the concept of distribution itself (should a copy of this or that go to 'Chaplains' or 'Education' or 'Welfare'?). Many were the flashes of colour which relieved the khaki monotony of the well-cut 'bush jackets' and long trousers which had now replaced the ludicrous uniform that had made Major Balderton regard me as 'a character from Noël Coward'. I wore the red armband of the General Staff myself. But there were other armbands of different colours, as well as coloured tabs and hatbands marking the rank of full Colonel and above – purple for medical, green for dentistry and pale blue for education, the last two being real collectors' items. Not many people, I imagine, have ever met a full Colonel of the Education Corps. Even in remote, obscure Central Command that organis-ation was beginning the work of indoctrination among the forces which was to help, later on, to secure a landslide victory for the Labour Party and the sensational ousting of Winston Churchill. Even then, I think, it was clear to me what these people were up to. It disturbed and alarmed me. So, in the larger world, did the close collaboration of Churchill, Roosevelt and Stalin and the enormous amount of support the Western Allies were giving the Russian Communist forces, enabling them to turn the Germans back and go on to an offensive which was not to end until they had occupied the eastern half of Europe. But on the whole I kept my own counsel. I had no more scenes with Major Atherstone-Smith. He would probably have refused to stay in the same room with me now that I was offending him not only by my political views but by my low moral standards.

The second winter of my life in India was beginning. The perfect weather came round again, as regular as clockwork. The nights were cold enough for fires (an additional charm for love-making). It was also a good time to go 'on tour' and that is what I was now doing, visiting subsidiary headquarters and units throughout the area which stretched from Lucknow in the Punjab to the borders of Hyderabad in the south and included, in the Central Provinces, the enchanted jungles and mountains of the Vindhya and the Satpura. My work – whatever it may have been – also meant that unlike most British or even Indian Army officers I met a great many Indian civilians. Ordered by Major Balderton and others to regard such people as not merely unspeakable but almost nonexistent, I now found that I could get on very well with them. They were fond of jokes, for one thing. They were not so much conservative as immovable, taking it for granted that as far as their daily lives were concerned nothing would ever change.

This applied particularly to Hindus, who, however westernised, still observed the ancient ceremonies and lived by the intricate rules of the caste system, with its multitude of sub-castes and sub-sub-castes underlying the pattern of the four great castes which, originally based on *varna*, colour, the light-skinned ancient Aryan conquerors of India had devised (or had it devised them?) to keep themselves aloof from the dark-skinned aboriginal inhabitants.

Just as Catholics can joke about their religion so, I found, could Hindus joke about their caste system. It is not, of course, a class system, nor is it based on money. This means, in principle, that it can never change, and it explains why, even now, Hindu India still has the only social system in the world which has not been absorbed or taken over by western liberalism and technology. No wonder I found it so attractive. And the system, so abhorrent to progressive people, had odd results which amused and enchanted me as much as the Hindus themselves.

One day, the Indian officer in our castle of indolence in Agra, now free of its wickerwork cooling apparatus, asked a clerk who was a Brahmin and of higher caste than himself to get him a glass of water. This he did unthinkingly. The officer, taking the glass, burst out laughing. 'Now you have defiled yourself! You, a Brahmin, have brought me, a Vaidhya, a glass of water. Now you must go to the temple and pay ten rupees to get yourself purified!' The Brahmin clerk, though somewhat mortified, also laughed and for a few moments the pair of them went through an elaborate ritual of oblique head-movements and spiral motions of the forearm. But the clerk, although he appreciated the joke, certainly did go and get himself purified. It would have been unthinkable not to do so.

When I think of that time, a multitude of dreamlike scenes come into my mind. With a congenial fellow-officer, who belonged to a

Gurkha regiment but was on attachment to the staff and became, for the time he was in Agra, a good friend and companion, I bicycled the short distance to the Taj Mahal several times and saw its ivory splendour, already familiar, perhaps too familiar, by moonlight and by flaming sunset. For all its beauty it did not produce the always hoped for numinous feeling. I was worried about this. Was this the end of youth? I was now in my thirtieth year, and to a man of thirty that already seems the beginning of age.

I peer through the wrong end of the telescope again. Now I am in Lucknow, city of poetry, music and gardens, drinking tea with a mysterious Muslim merchant in the main room of his big, yellow-brown mansion, hidden behind high, dung-coloured walls and a thick, iron-studded doorway in an obscure alleyway smelling of mingled urine, incense and wood-smoke. We talk, and as we talk there is a continual giggling and whispering behind the elaborate lattice screen which runs along one end of the room. 'Please pay no attention,' he says. 'It is the women. They are curious about you.' He gets up now and again, excusing himself with elaborate courtesy, goes behind the screen of the zenana and bids his wives – he has four, the maximum allowed by Islamic law, denoting that, unlike most Muslim, he is rich enough to maintain them – remember their manners. But the giggling and whispering soon begin again. I have an impression of dark eyes peering through the interstices of the screen.

Later that evening we dine in my hotel, set in splendid gardens and with as fine a collection of turbaned, soft-footed servants as any old-fashioned novelist could imagine. Then he takes me to a concert. It is in the open air, in a garden where the faint splash of fountains can be heard in the background of that music which is like no other. Strange, soothing, hypnotic, the concert goes on all through the warm night, under the big stars, as various players of sitar, dilruba, tablas and so on, as well as singers and reciters, come and go, and members of the audience also come and go. Vividly coloured mineral water, bright green, scarlet, purple, orange but all tasting the same, intolerably sweet, as Indians like it, are on sale, together with sugar balls, pan, betel nut and various other substances which Indians maintain, no doubt rightly, are 'beneficial to blood'. It is as unlike a European concert as can be imagined. Listening to the sonorities of that music, insidious and seductive, making our Western music seem, for the moment, noisy and square-cut by comparison, and even crass, I am enslaved. I am still there as the subtly coloured Indian dawn invades the sky and the sun rises quickly for another hot English summer day.

Now I am in the big tent, carpeted like the tents of the Mogul court as it made its way from Delhi to Kashmir, of an officers' mess in some training area in the jungle, enjoying the drinks and jokes – some at the expense of 'staff wallahs' – and surprised, perhaps, to find that some unlikely Indian Army officer has not only done some quite tolerable water-colours in his spare moments but has a copy of 'A Shropshire Lad' in his pocket and knows most of it by heart.

I stop my truck by the roadside in some remote place in the jungle in order to relieve myself among the trees. I hear a flute playing in the distance. There is a fine waterfall, sunny glades, fallen leaves. A path leads down into the forest. I follow it a short way, tempted for a moment to go further, find the flute-player, join the aboriginal tribe which lives somewhere in this paradise, wed one or more of their slender women. What an utterly stupid idea! I go back to the road and my driver looks at me curiously as I order him to proceed. To him this is the abode of savages, deadly snakes, wild beasts, the terrible wild bees which nest in the crevices of the red, sandstone cliffs – a place to get away from as soon as possible.

Now I am walking in some godforsaken military camp somewhere in the great Gangetic Plain, talking to who knows what bewildered brigadier about the state of public opinion (what can that possibly mean in Indian terms?) in Cawnpore or Allahabad; about the Indian National Army; how many people have heard of it or sympathise with it; how, if at all, they get news of it (I have been listening, perhaps, to English-language broadcasts by the Japanese radio in Burma and heard a march-past of detachments from the nations of the Greater East Asia Co-Prosperity Sphere, 'Eight Corners under one Roof', which sounds like a parody of a Nuremberg rally coming from another planet); and my eyes stray to the great river with its shoals and sandy islands, whose further shore, two miles away, I cannot distinguish from the mists of evening.

I am accompanying a party of visiting Afghan generals round military installations and ammunition factories. None speak more than a few words of English. Some have done a course at the Potsdam Military Academy and speak some German. Had the Germans entered India, as it had seemed they might have done less than a year before, these well-mannered Afghans would have raised no great objection; now they know which is going to be the winning side. One speaks of his love of Persian poetry; invites me, when the war is over, to stay with him in Kabul and see his rose gardens. What Communist gun-emplacement occupies those gardens now? And what would he have said if he had known that many years after, one of the results of the war would be the destruction of his own country?

Towards the end of February 1944 I went with a party of Indian newspaper editors to the 'Forgotten Front' on the border of India and Burma. It included one Englishman, the agreeable editor of the *Civil and Military Gazette* of Lahore, Kipling's old paper, among a dozen or so Indians, mostly editors of vernacular papers. We foregathered in Calcutta; then travelled by a very slow train to Dimapur on the Ganges, crossing the great river (I did not fail to remind myself that it had flowed out of Tibet) by ferry and staying in a base-camp which because of the great number of *lingams*, stone phallic symbols, to be seen round about, was called by the British soldiery 'Penis Park'. From there we went by road to Kohima and Imphal, headquarters of the Fourth Indian Army, a beautiful place in a lunar crater surrounded by forests and jagged mountains. To reach it we had to drive perilously on serpentine roads hacked out of precipices by gangs of tribal labourers who worked continuously to repair sections cut by landslides. At certain places could be seen, a thousand feet down, the rusting burned out wrecks of trucks just like our own.

I got on pretty well with these Indian editors, who, though at first suspicious, responded well to teasing and fantasy. There was trouble one morning when one of them came to me complaining that one of the others had stolen his watch. I ordered them all to 'parade' before me, then told them that if they did not behave themselves I would have them all taken to a quarry and shot. This greatly amused them. But it was not long before the editor whose watch was missing told me that it had mysteriously reappeared. One of the others looked sheepish and avoided my eye. What, I wondered, would Major Balderton have said to this? Would he have given his mad, cackling laugh? I doubt it.

The weather was still quite cool and the mountain air intoxicating. We drove eastward, over roads even more hair-raising, to Tamu, just on the border. It was deserted. All around were mountainous green forests of paradisial beauty. To the east those forests held the Japanese enemy.

Back in Imphal I found my friend Richard Storry, now attached to headquarters as a Japanese expert and interrogator of such Japanese as allowed themselves to be taken prisoner. At the moment there was only one, a wounded man brought back unconscious from a patrol. I looked at him with curiosity. He would say nothing, but only demanded the means of killing himself to avoid dishonour. We dined with the amusing Resident in Imphal, a 'Native State' with an eccentric Rajah; it was all immensely civilised, in a remote part of the Raj, where not even rumours of possible independence had penetrated and the names of Gandhi and Nehru were scarcely known.

We flew back next month in a rickety old Dakota from the Imphal airstrip. As we waited to board the plane I noted that it had brought, on its flight from Calcutta, an eminent personage. It was Orde Wingate, newly created Major-General, Churchill's protégé, inventor of the Chindits, the Long Range Penetration Groups which operated far behind the Japanese lines, with the loss of many lives and with dubious results. The General did not know it any more than we did, but he was on his last journey. A little later he was fated to die in an air crash in the Burmese jungle – his disappearance not entirely unwelcome to the orthodox generals he had overridden with what they thought of, perhaps rightly, as his hare-brained schemes.

I watched this famous personage with fascination. He looked every bit as eccentric as his reputation had it: a tall, gaunt figure in a pith helmet (was he the very last soldier to wear one?); a book (the Bible? Clausewitz? *The Oxford Book of English Verse?*) under one arm; in one hand a blue flower of a species unknown to me. All went in awe of him. He was said, among other things, to sit outside his tent in the evenings shooting at wasps with his revolver. I was glad I was not under his command, I reflected, as we flew creakingly westward over the floodlands of East Bengal (the pilot could not resist an ancient joke at the expense of non-flyers: 'Hold on to your hats; one engine gone; but I think with a bit of luck we'll just make it').

Back in Agra, in the dreamland of Central Command, tired and dirty from the journey, I was met by eager Harriet as if I were a hero. I had hardly time to take off my revolver-belt before she had got me into bed. Next day there were two items of news. One came from my mother, a telegram dated a month before, telling me that my father, who had been suffering from leukemia for several months, had died. The other news was that the Japanese, in those beautiful jungles I had just been looking at, had started their long-prepared offensive, their last throw of the war, as it turned out, and had begun to cut the roads leading to Imphal. 'Bad luck, Wharton,' said some aged Brigadier, 'you've just missed all the fun.'

It was not long before Imphal was almost surrounded, unreachable except by air, and the bloody battle of Kohima, where I had sat not long ago admiring the scenery from the balcony of the comfortable *dak* bungalow, was providing all the fun of that sort which anybody could wish for. The 'Forgotten Front' was forgotten no longer. But once again, by a curious chance, I had just left a place where the most horrific things were about to happen for a place where nothing much happened at all.

Now it was March and the fine North Indian winter was over. It grew hotter and more trying every day. As it grew hotter Harriet grew colder, to me at any rate, for I think this fickle and animated woman had not been without suitors during the month I had been away. Her first warm welcome turned to tiresomeness and recrimination, then to positive aloofness. She had taken up with some young major or other and although I did not love her or value her very much except as an agreeable bed and drinking companion, I felt pangs of jealousy greater than I have ever felt before or since. I debased myself, made myself foolish, lost my temper in public, wept in private, knowing, of course, that if I had any hope of getting her back this was the most certain way of losing it. There was, of course, though I did not think of it at the time, an excellent remedy for this humiliating experience. I could have 'wangled' my way back to my regiment, then in the thick of the fighting on the Burma Front. It was what the heroes of romantic novels did, and what was sometimes done even in real life. But I was no hero.

Instead of being a hero, I went on a month's leave to Kashmir, pining at first and caring nothing for the privilege of being in a place which to people back in England and Yorkshire was a fabulous paradise ('Pale hands I loved beside the Shalimar' – Mrs Woodford-Finden's 'Four Indian Love Lyrics' were one of the very few pieces of recorded music in my parents' house). I thought about my father, of how I had been brought to misjudge a man whose bursts of lunatic bad temper were perfectly explicable and whose underlying goodness, generosity and even humour I had understood so little. I had a thoroughly morbid time.

After a bit I bestirred myself, went out to see the sights of the place (including the Shalimar Garden with its stone pavilions, formal flower-beds, fountains, rills and strutting hoopoes). I con-soled myself as best I could with an officer's wife I can hardly remember. It was not a good leave. My pretence to myself that I was gathering material for a novel about the Public Relations Directorate was not convincing, though I made a lot of notes of oddities of behaviour, coincidences and inane remarks. I also thought of writing an *Anatomy of Boredom*, on the lines of Burton's *Anatomy of Melancholy*, and made some notes on this fascinating subject on which I was so well qualified to write. But the more I thought about it the more mysterious and unfathomable it seemed. It would be necessary to trace it back to the time, if time it could be called, before the Fall of the Rebel Angels. It would be necessary to deal with all aspects of Accidie, the deadly sin of which, out of all the deadly sins, I was most guilty. The prevalence of Accidie in mediaeval monasteries, where the monks must have drowsed away on summer afternoons, fuddled on the strong ale of which, accord-ing to the records, they had such a generous allowance ... no wonder the manuscripts they were supposed to be copying were full of textual corruptions which hundreds of years later were to delight the rigorous mind of Professor Housman ... The sin of Accidie, alone, I thought, was a lifetime's study, and that was only one strand in the great *Anatomy of Boredom* ...

When I returned to the intolerable plains of India and to what must, I suppose, be called the real world, the war had moved into a new phase. D-Day had come and the Allies were in France. The Japanese were in retreat and our own Army, commanded by General Slim, the admirable soldier whose maps I had once had the privilege of marking up with my chinagraph pencil, was on the offensive at last. It was fortunate that Wingate, favourite of Churchill, that very bad judge of men who had taken against the admirable Auchinleck and Wavell, was not around to interfere and even, it might be, oust the admirable Slim and claim the credit for victory. For once justice prevailed and the credit went to the one man who deserved it.

From Europe the news was both good and bad. It was good that the Nazis were being defeated. But it was bad, I thought, that the Allies were insisting on 'unconditional surrender'. We heard, perhaps some time after the event, details of the Plot of July 20, of Hitler's escape, of the hideous fate of Stauffenberg and the other heroic Germans who had tried to save their country not only from the Nazis but from the Russian Communists. Was I the only officer in the whole British Army in India who raged against their betrayal, our own failure to help the German Resistance, our rulers' refusal, for whatever reason, even to admit that there *was* a German Resistance?

Soon I was posted to Eastern Army HQ in Calcutta and took my torpor, melancholia and occasional bouts of activity to a billet in the Great Eastern Hotel in Chowringhee, the main street of that atrocious city, with its pullulating slums, its trams hung with white-clad clerks like swarming insects, its sacred cows nuzzling among the vegetable stalls to claim their portion (and what Hindu dare deny them?) and flop down in the middle of the street, obstructing the traffic until they chose, perhaps to oblige some soft-voiced, exceptionally pious devotee, to move; its two fantastic railway stations, Howrah and Sealdah, whose platforms were the only home of thousands of near-starving people, their innumerable children, the brass pots, ragged pallets and images of monkey or elephant gods which were all they owned.

To me, as to most Europeans (and not a few prosperous Indians) this world of fearful poverty and aimless bustle, of continual birth, sickness and death, was simply something 'given'. I did not grieve or agonise over these innumerable wretched human beings; I did not feel ashamed, when eating chocolate cake in Firpo's, the famous tea-shop, when a beggar woman held out her brass bowl. I would give her a few annas, fighting back the hideous joke which forced itself into my mind – to give her chocolate cake instead. I did not even blench when I saw dead bodies by the roadside, any more than did the Indians walking or bicycling past (sometimes, such was the sinuous agility of these narrow-boned people, with three or four on the same bicycle). To them it was a common sight. Next day the bodies would have been removed, not perhaps before the kitehawks always circling overhead made their obscene investigations.

Most of my time in Calcutta seemed to be spent in pointless conferences on this and that. With the end of the war now clearly in sight, the question of India's future began to emerge and become inescapable. I learned something of Indian opinion from people who often showed an uncanny prescience of what was going to happen. I did a half-hour weekly broadcast commentary on the progress of the war. Whether anybody listened to it I never discovered.

My Gurkha friend at Agra had given me an introduction to an agreeable English family, whose father was in the ICS. There were two beautiful and intelligent daughters. The younger was about twenty years old, a student of Indian dancing and music. I grew particularly fond of her and would have been madly in love if she had given the least sign of encouragement. But I was never good at seduction, except of women I had no respect for. Her wise, half-laughing gravity delighted me, but I would not have dreamed – at least do anything more than dream – of laying a finger on her. Now thirty-one, I thought myself far too old for this magical being.

So we were friends. I even found I could tell her about the secret of the Missing Will and the mysterious Curse of the Whartons. She came to dinner with me occasionally at the Great Eastern Hotel, which as well as billeting staff officers, was also the main hotel of Calcutta, full of bustle and confusion. I felt the absurd pride of being seen by fellow-officers with this beautiful young girl.

That May the war in Europe ended. As the hot weather drew towards its intolerable climax I was posted to GHQ New Delhi and employed on propaganda work as well as editing an Army magazine, in which I printed some of my own surrealist stories. Here I found some congenial people in the great, swarming anthill of GHQ not far from the Viceroy's House in Lutyens's glorious, spacious capital. My old acquaintance Major Rankin, he of the chemical warfare, was now an assistant secretary to the Viceroy, the admirable, eccentric Lord Wavell, whom Churchill had treated so badly, evidently mistrusting an obviously honest man. So I did not want for dinner parties and drinks parties with some of the great ones of the earth, from the Viceroy, the amiable and civilised Wavell, downwards. But for the drink which the overwhelmingly charming, well-mannered and mischievous Rankin thoughtfully provided in admirable quantity, these people would probably have terrified me to death.

As usual, I often wondered why I was here and what exactly I was doing. It was my passivity, my tendency to drift with the stream, to take the easy way, to be acted upon rather than act which had brought me here. But I could hardly complain or say I found it intolerable when, on a clear, starlit night I sat with Rankin and other friends in the Mughal Garden of the Viceroy's House, hearing the splash of fountains and the distant rumble of the city, drinking delicious drinks, talking agreeable nonsense and in the end – I was addicted to the habit – falling asleep.

There were many other transitory friends – George Wyndham of the ICS and his wife, the artist 'Haro' Hodson, his cousin Anne

Richmond, an intelligent, attractive girl with remarkably fine green eyes and some literary talent, who had joined a special corps of women designed to operate in the recaptured territories of the Far East as the Japanese were pushed back. She was a heroine indeed. Her reason for joining the corps was to be able to greet her fiancé, David Piper, when he was released from the Japanese prison-camp where he had been since the fall of Singapore. All turned out as she hoped and their story had a happy ending.

Meanwhile preparations were going on at GHQ for the British part in the final act of the war – the comparatively humble one of retaking Singapore, Malaya, the Dutch East Indies and Indo-China. One of those who were working on these plans was Brigadier Enoch Powell, already a byword for his terrifying and meticulous efficiency and his habit of wearing service dress, Sam Browne belt and all, in the hot weather, after the fashion of his predecessors in the Army of the East India Company. To the majority of the staff, who were flopping about in bush shirts, he seemed a formidable eccentric. It was rumoured (correctly) that he read Thucydides and that his ambition was to be Viceroy of India (which, if there were any justice in this world, he would have been). But there was to be no British attack on the Dutch East Indies, or anywhere else. One August evening news came over the wireless that an atomic bomb had been dropped on Japan.

The war was over. It is hard to remember what I and the people I knew felt about the way it ended. There was both shock and relief – relief that the war was over, and shock that technology had moved into another, even more utterly inhuman dimension. There was a victory parade for 'VJ Day' in Delhi as elsewhere. But there was no wild rejoicing. The dismantling of the European empires (with the exception of the Soviet Empire) was about to begin, eagerly abetted by the Americans, whose late President Roosevelt had not been one of my favourites, and the British Raj was clearly high up on the list. Bad news came thick and fast. At the General Election in England the Labour party had won a landslide victory, bemoaned by me and my friends but, as I could not help noticing, received with glee by many of my fellow-officers. They were of the sort who, through the Army Education Corps and other agencies, had been working away steadily throughout the war to bring about this outcome. I learned of it with despair, believing, in my pessimistic way, that there could never be another Conservative Government in England. Nor was there, in my own sense of the word 'conservative', which my experiences in the Army and my 'reactionary' views, reinforced by contact with intelligent Indians and others, had confirmed.

I was offered the choice of going to Japan for a year as part of the somewhat pathetic British contingent of the slightly less pathetic Commonwealth contingent of the Allied but almost entirely American forces of occupation, or taking my turn to await demobilisation, which would mean another six months or so in India. Unenterprisingly, I chose the latter. Or perhaps I was not being entirely unenterprising. I had been in the Army for five years and was beginning to have the feeling I had had about Oxford, that I had always been in it, always would be and that there was no world outside it. It was necessary to realize that there was. It was time I got back to England and decided what to do with the rest of my life.

I was made up to Lieutenant-Colonel (Temporary) and sent to join the staff of Southern Command at Bangalore. The next six months would have been a sort of prolonged holiday if it had not been for the fact that the Indians, both Hindu and Muslim, were now beginning to press for independence with the certainty that in some form or other they were soon going to get it. The 'Quit India' movement revived. Even in Bangalore, an agreeable place where I soon found agreeable company, I sometimes came across small groups of Indians carrying banners and saying politely 'Quit India, please'. Averse to change of any kind, I was not in favour of this but believed the Raj should go on for ever, if only on the grounds that it was much more agreeable for everybody than anything likely to succeed it. My Indian friends did not agree. Even the Begum ————, a member of an ancient landowning family in the North-West Frontier Province who had angered them by leaving her husband, did not agree with me on this point, though she did on many others. She was a Junior Commander (equivalent to Captain) in the IAF and occasionally wore a khaki-coloured uniform sari which became her only a little less than any of the dozens of beautiful saris she possessed.

I had originally met her through my friend Stuart Daniel, who was also a Staff Lieutenant-Colonel at the Southern Command H Q. I had known him vaguely at Oxford. At week-ends, with other congenial people, British and Indian, we went for elaborate picnics in the country around Bangalore, which was flat, with sensational rocky outcrops about as high above the plain as the hills of the Lake District are above sea-level, often with temples on top. We climbed some of these, bravely careless of thorn-trees, snakes and wild beasts. The Begum, whose duties in the Army seemed to be purely ceremonial, had two family retainers with her. One was a fierce-looking man who, had she ordered it, would have instantly cut a man's head off without more ado, and a serving woman almost as fierce-looking, who always carried an enormous iron spoon for dealing with beggars and other importunate people.

One week-end we spent in a comfortable bungalow on the Nandi Hills, where Tippoo Sahib had had an almost impregnable fort, as well as a convenient precipice for dropping prisoners over. It was said that one prisoner, a Scottish soldier, had survived the 500-foot drop to tell the tale. Now, on this shady hill which was like a small garden of Eden, we ate, drank and talked next to the very wall which must once have heard the screams of struggling victims.

When not engaged in these parties of pleasure I went on tours which took me to Madras and various other places including, for some reason I cannot remember, Golconda and the small French colony of Pondicherry, where I met the Governor, an impenetrable Frenchman in a superb uniform of a fashion already doomed. Beneath the surface of this life of Reilly, violence was lurking. The Indian National Army, which had surrendered on the Japanese defeat, was granted pardon en masse (to the great indignation of many), but its members, even if they merely returned to their native villages, had learned the lesson that the British could be defied. At the Bangalore headquarters we practised revolver-shooting.

It was in February 1946, when my time in India was running out, that news came of the Indian Naval Mutiny at Bombay, where the ratings, disarming their officers, had taken over several ships and *had actually turned their guns on the Bombay Yacht Club.* 'Beggars couldn't hit a gasometer if they were standing inside it,' said some old colonel. But he was speaking out of a world which had already passed away. Rioting broke out in Bombay, where, as in all Indian cities, there were masses of people with nothing much to do who always welcomed the chance of a good riot. These *goondas*, as they are called, made a point of seizing mineral water factories for the sake of their bottles of fizzy drinks, which had excellent fragmentation on impact. For a day or so the city was in their hands; the Congress leaders themselves became alarmed at the demon they had raised up; and finding their appeals in vain called on the Army to restore order, which it did with much greater loss of humble lives than ever was reported in the Press.

When I flew to Bombay to join the emergency headquarters which had been set up the worst of the trouble (of course) was over. Proceeding in convoy from the airfield to headquarters (I had been asked to take special care of some cases of whisky for the General) we came under a certain amount of stoning, and I even felt called upon to fire my revolver in the air, more in surprise than anger. After a day or two of intensive conferences, map-marking, drawing up contingency plans and other military activities, the city was pacified, the mutineers disarmed.

I returned to Bangalore and cancelling a projected 'tour' of Ceylon, set off with Stuart Daniel and the Begum for a fortnight's holiday in Ootacamund. 'Ooty' was, and no doubt still is, a place out of a fairy story – a region of rolling hills very much like the Wiltshire Downs as they must have been at the beginning of this century, but on a vast scale and including curious waterfalls and exotic flowers not to be found in Wiltshire. Being about 5,000 feet above sea-level, this paradise had the climate of a perfect English summer. The Begum had several English friends here and my friend Stuart soon contrived to captivate one of their attractive young daughters. It was typical of me that although the Begum was more interesting and in her own way quite as attractive, I hankered after this other girl and was quite put out when the time came for us to leave. Stuart decided to stay on for another week with his new sweetheart. The Begum and I, with her two servants, the serving woman brandishing her iron spoon more fiercely than ever, took the bus down the mountain in a sensationally coloured sunset to the railhead for Bangalore.

But now all was changed. The date for my departure had been fixed. Amid some lamentations I sorted out the clutter of objects I had accumulated during the last five years, took leave of my fellow-officers, shook the General's hand, had ritual garlands of jasmine draped about my neck by Indian clerks and servants and then on an appointed night boarded the train which was to take me and others to the transit camp at Devlali, famous for inducing the special brand of lunacy called 'Doolali tap'. Heaven knows what promises I made to the Begum, who proposed in due course to follow me to England. All proved false.

Devlali did not make me any more lunatic than I already was, but the fortnight or so I spent waiting there, eating appalling food and drinking appalling liquor, relieved only by a visit to Poona, to whose magnificent club I still owe twenty rupees for unredeemed bar-chits, was trying enough. The next stage was Bombay, where I somehow contrived to stay at the Taj Mahal Hotel, sitting alone on its westward terrace which looked over the sea, drinking gin and reading with complacent sadness a book which suited my elegiac mood, Cyril Connolly's just published *The Unquiet Grave*, bought at Tapoorewala'a bookshop for four rupees. Now India and everything I had done and seen there began to recede, grow small, closed off, turn into material for nostalgia: the forests, the mountains, the mad laugh of Major Balderton, my Muslim friend in Lucknow, with his wives and music, the corpse in the bazaar, the eyes of a magical girl, Wavell the deaf and agreeable Viceroy, soon to be succeeded by the preposterous Mountbatten, the snows of Kanchenjunga, Wingate with his book and flower, the lunar landscape of Imphal, the elephant in the jungle, the furtive loves of Agra and Simla, Mitsutachi the imaginary general, the wide streets of Imperial Delhi with their hundred thousand bicycles . . .

All was reversed: my arrival at Bombay in 1942 became my departure in 1946. I went aboard, but the ship was no civilised, class-divided *Orion*. Something had been happening in the world while I had been away. It was the irresistible advance of democracy. No longer were the soldiers battened below decks. Now they would have mutinied in earnest. As it was they grumbled, not with the old grumbling but with a new rancour. Their womenfolk, many indoctrinated in hatred of the 'officer class', did more than merely grumble. All ranks in the crowded ship messed together in relays. I had left England a Second Lieutenant, sharing a comfortable cabin with three others. I returned a Major, sharing an uncomfortable cabin with half a dozen others. And, since America had conquered and imposed its will on England in small matters as in great, there was not in all that troopship a single drop of alcohol to drink.

What did I expect to find, or expect to do, as we crossed the

Indian Ocean, entered the Red Sea, with its dark green waters and jagged mountains, almost the only potent image which stays with me from that voyage, so much shorter yet more tedious than the voyage out; moved through the phantasmagoria of Port Said and into a calm, misty, ghostly Mediterranean; glimpsed the Rock; passed into the Atlantic where U-boats lurked no longer, saw the first of England, the Isle of Wight; landed at Southampton on or about my thirty-third birthday?

5
Attlee and After

The docks looked grey and battered and shabby; the people too. Not a single family, I found, was living among brass vessels, brightly-coloured cloths and household gods on the platforms of Southampton station. Not a single coolie hung dreamily about, waiting to carry something or perform some other service for an anna or a farthing. At the tops of walls there were a lot of elementary, childlike drawings of the same round face – 'Chad', the character who seemed to stand for England in its present state, with chalked slogans: 'Wot – no cigarettes?' 'Wot – no women?' It was all extremely strange. After a period of confusion, compounded of the Army 'fuck up' I was accustomed to and a new kind of civilian inefficiency, a party of us, still in uniform but already feeling the bewilderment of change, entrained, travelled with many un-explained stops – that at least was like the country I had come from – through a damp, green, miniature landscape to Tilehurst near Reading, where we were to spend the night before dispersing to various demobilisation centres. We drank beer in a pub and felt like ghosts.

As the only address I had to go to was in Dublin – my wife, who had a married sister in the neutral Irish Free State, had moved there some time before – my demobilisation centre was at Ashton-under-Lyne, near Stockport in the Manchester Conurbation. After a day's travelling through more of this unfamiliar miniature country full of houses, I reached that unattractive place. Next morning I filled in a lot of forms and collected some 'demob' clothes – I noted that they were the same for officers and men. I chose a tweed jacket, grey flannel trousers, brown shoes with bright brass eyes. In a few minutes, as it seemed, I was a civilian again. But I still wore my uniform, unwilling to take the final step into a confusing world where I had no definite, acknowledged place, as though my time in the Army had never been.

Feeling more than ever like a ghost, I spent the night at an hotel in Chester after a day of aimless sightseeing in that city, where I had never been before. In the cool, grey spring weather I walked by the Dee, watched at a certain place how the swans came sailing over the green water to where the dustmen of Chester had stopped their lorries and were throwing handfuls of stale bread to the beautiful, greedy birds. I made a note. I was always making notes for future books; but where was the will to write them?

It was late on the following day when I reached Dublin. The station seemed deserted. Holding my suitcase – the rest of my baggage would (or would not) follow later, I stood irresolutely. Then I saw a single horse-cab waiting. My wife and son – now eight years old – were there. What did I feel – what did she feel – what, for that matter, did he feel – at this statutory moment of reunion? Very little, I think. We went back to the flat she had, somewhere near Merrion Square, talked, I suppose, ate some supper, I suppose, and went to bed. I tried to make love to her. It was a failure.

I spent a few weeks in Dublin, living on my gratuity, which then seemed quite a respectable sum. I had a growing feeling, and so, of course, had she, that this would not do. I was bored, ill-tempered, tried to write, failed. We quarrelled a good deal and I decided to leave for England. I had nowhere to go except to my brother's farm near Ambleside in the Lake District, where my widowed mother was living. She seemed much older and smaller when she met me at Windermere station, resplendent in my uniform with a major's crowns still on my shoulders. My brother, who seemed to have done quite well out of the war – he had a much more civilised farmhouse in a not particularly remote place and even had a sign in the window: 'Teas' – soon cut me down to size. 'It's always the useless ones who survive,' he muttered. He may well have been right. But what, I wondered, had become of my *Encyclopaedia Britannica*, my bicycle, my maps and my Greek lexicon, the only things of value I had left behind?

The atmosphere was not congenial. The old antagonism between my mother and her daughter-in-law had not changed. 'I won't be treated like a servant', 'that clock is really mine.' Such remarks as these were common. My mother told me, not once but many times, that she had sold much of the remaining treasure of 'Duchy Grange' – the silver, a fine emerald ring she had – to help my brother stock his farm: 'and look at all the thanks I get'. After a bit I felt I could not stand any more of this. I would give Dublin another try. I sent my wife a telegram to say I was coming back. The sweet, romantic soul replied with a telegram in overwrought, romantic terms, which, intercepted by my brother, greatly embarrassed me. But off I went.

This time it did not take me long to realise I had made yet another mistake. It would not do. I had grown so far apart from my wife and had so little feeling for her or my child that I must leave. On a fine day of midsummer I crossed the Irish Sea once more and this time caught the express from Holyhead to London. An Army friend – a 'mad Irishman' with an MC and two bars who, angry at not being awarded the DSO, had once upset the mess dining-table over his CO – had arranged a room for me in a bed-sitter house in Ebury Street. It was a tiny attic, with just enough room for a narrow bed, a table and chair and a spluttering gas fire. I was entirely alone.

Now began a very dreary and depressing time. I walked the Chelsea streets, hoping, perhaps, to meet someone I had known who would somehow lead me back to the old life. I ate abominable meals – they had the very taste of 'austerity' – in abominable pubs or in cheap cafés. I went to The Antelope, off Eaton Square – it had been a favourite haunt in what had become 'the old days'.

There, for want of anyone else to talk to I fell in with a set of men and women – the men, like me, were living on their dwindling gratuities – who had little in common with me except a liking for drink and a feeling of being lost in the civilian world.

My money was running out. It was necessary to get a job. I applied for various posts, including one as a Public Relations Officer with the new National Waste Paper Board (can this be right?). I have never been good at interviews. This one was particularly farcical. As I sat before the interviewers, answering various questions, I could see their puzzlement that I, who had lately held the rank of colonel, should seem so totally unfitted for any job at all. My handkerchief had escaped through a hole in my pocket. As I rose to go ('we'll let you know soon') I made a grab at the handkerchief through the hole and seized it, but then, trying to withdraw my arm, found my cuff caught in the hole. I scrambled crablike to the door, and as I closed it behind me, heard the roar of laughter from the other side. A good film sequence, I thought, and even made a note.

Other interviews were less amusing. A terrible torpor fell upon me. I spent hours lying without thought on the narrow bed in my attic hide-out. I even wrote a letter to my wife in Dublin, suggesting that we should get together again. Wisely, she declined. Chance led me, one despairing evening, to the pub in Rathbone Place, off Oxford Street, where I had originally met Constantine FitzGibbon. Perhaps I hoped to meet him again. Instead I met the instrument of my deliverance, my old friend of Oxford days, David Thomson.

He was still the same delightful, vague, generous and unselfconscious man he had been then, though he was more mature and confident from experience, as I may have at least appeared to be. He was with three beautiful Irish sisters and seemed to be in love with all of them and they, perhaps, with him. Because of his bad sight he had not served in the forces but had done farming and later joined the BBC. He was now a producer and writer in its 'features' department, which was responsible for documentary programmes. Finding that I was looking for work, he suggested that I should write a programme in a series he was producing by writers new to the 'radio medium'. Any subject I liked, he said in his vague way. I chose the Reading Room of the British Museum and with much toil and agony (I have always greatly disliked writing) eventually produced a somewhat over-poetic script which was broadcast, complete with sound effects, background music from Holst's 'Planets' and so on, towards the end of the year.

Very soon my deliverer introduced me to his colleagues and friends. The BBC then, as now, was distributed all over London; the Features Department had its offices near 'BH', as I soon learned to call the shiplike building, huge by the standards of that time, in Portland Place. The Department, whose chief was Lawrence Gilliam, a big, powerfully-built man with grey hair curly as a negro's, was then at the height of its fame. It was regarded by other parts of the BBC as something of a spoilt child. Because it included people of talent and was headed by a man who was fiercely loyal to them and protected them, it was allowed to go very much its own way. It therefore got good results – 'classics' of sound radio which seem now to belong to a remote epoch. It provided writers like Louis MacNeice, Rayner Heppenstall and W. R. ('Bertie') Rodgers with a living wage. On the other hand it was a danger to them. It was easier for them to use their talents in the evanescent medium of radio than to write books. Much good writing must have been lost that way.

The Features Department's own pub was The Stag's Head, on the corner of Hallam Street and Great Cavendish Street. Here I met Francis Dillon, or 'Jack', as he was always called, a small, energetic, semi-edentate man who kept up a continuous quickfire of jokes, often very good ones, in a high, hoarse voice (he had been gassed in the First World War). Because of his shabby appearance and ungentlemanly accent I took him at first for an unusually privileged member of the manual staff, a driver, perhaps (the spell of the Army was still on me). I could not have been more wrong. He was a man of great talent, who put most of it into talking and singing in pubs (he was an authority on folk-songs) rather than into books, or even into his official work. At that time he was editing and producing 'Country Magazine', a popular programme which went out at Sunday lunchtime on what was then called (in contradistinction to the 'Light Programme') the 'Home Service'. It was full of country lore, poachers, eccentric beekeepers, fragments of a rural England which still, even in 1946, somehow survived.

Before long I was doing odd jobs for this programme, earning just about enough to live on by interviewing country characters, writing down what they would say on the air (there were no tape-recorders in those days) and generally fitting their contributions into the final script. I did other jobs for other programmes, too – anything that was going, in fact. I wrote scripts for the Schools Programme on the Luddites (a theme always close to my heart) and soon became familiar with the simple techniques of the studio from red light to stopwatch.

'*Narrator*: By 1818 the condition of the handloom-weavers, betrayed, as they believed, by the new machines, became desperate: (Fade up murmuring crowd)
'*Voice 1*: Give us bread!
'*Voice 2*: We're starvin'!
'*Voice 3 (female)*: Our children are starvin'!
(Loud angry murmur, clang of mill gates)
'*Voice 1*: Smash the frames!
'*Voice 2*: Aye, smash the devil's frames!
etc. etc.'

I also wrote, on the other hand, scripts about modern industries and things of that kind, my greatest masterpiece being 'Focus on Waste Paper' – an important subject in the years of austerity, rationing, 'Work or Want' and all the drab, grey phantasmagoria of Mr Attlee's Labour Government. The staff of the Features Department, if they had any political views at all, would have described themselves as mildly Socialist, I suppose, though there was a Marxist element represented by R. D. ('Reggie') Smith, a big, bearlike, kindly-looking man who had a neat trick of giving bores a helping hand and then neatly unloading them on someone else, occasionally myself.

As for 'austerity', why should a physically healthy man in his thirties, just out of the Army, worry about that? I met, while drinking in The Stag, an energetic, jolly, dark-haired, handsome Welsh girl called Anne who produced programmes about films. We set up house together in a flat in Hampstead conveniently offered by a friend of mine from post-Oxford days. His wife had been Constantine FitzGibbon's girl friend when he came to stay with us in Westmorland. The pair of them were on their way back to Nigeria, where he worked in the Colonial Service. It was in this flat that we lived through the dread winter of 1946–7, when the streets of London were covered with waves of black ice and were impassable to traffic for days on end. It was an 'offence' to use more than one bar of an electric fire and we had to drag bags of inferior coal, when we could get any, from the depot in Finchley Road up the slopes of Hampstead Hill. All our water-pipes froze and we cannot have had much to eat. But I remember nothing of this hardship; only the exhilaration when the thaw came at last and the huge long icicles which draped our walls, things of iridescent beauty, gradually disappeared.

Wishing to get a divorce, I consulted Stuart Daniel, he of Bangalore, now in chambers in London, and under his direction wrote the statutory letter to my wife in Dublin, saying that I had left her and was now living in adultery with so-and-so at such-and-such an address. In due course, a small, furtive man with a black notebook arrived one evening, just as in a thousand novels of the age before divorce became commonplace. 'I'll have to trouble you for evidence of co-habitation,' he said. 'If I could just look in the bedroom . . . If you could just lay out your . . . night attire on the bed . . . Thank you. No, I won't stay for a cup of coffee, thank you. I've three or four more calls to make tonight.' So it was done, and about nine months later, I was a single man. 'How do you feel?' asked Anne. 'Alone in the world,' I said.

She was a very energetic girl, determined, until she decided the task was hopeless, to see me 'make something of myself' and my presumed talents. It was she who fixed up a holiday for us in a château in the Valley of the Tarn, where, in the hot sun of the Midi, I became almost as brown as I had been in India; she who arranged another holiday in the Dordogne, then unpeopled by English settlers; she who worked things so that we could see the paintings in the cavern at Lascaux, before they were closed because of the destructive breath of too many visitors; she who arranged a few days in Paris, of which I remember little except a scene at the Gare du Nord, when we found ourselves, with a group of other English people, on the wrong platform. ''Raus! 'Raus!' shouted a French porter, to the huge amusement of his fellow countrymen and the indignation of the English. I thought it funny myself; Anne less so.

We were not really getting on well together. She had little patience with my listless and despondent moods. Why should she? I felt the odds and ends of work I was doing for the BBC were using only a small part of my capacity. 'Then why don't you write? You're supposed to be a writer.' But I could not. Remembering those solitary walks on Hampstead Heath when Anne was working and I was supposed to be writing some stupid script which I couldn't get started, that feeling of hopelessness combined with a powerful charge of unreality – I had not yet learned to call this sensation, subsequently so popular, *angst* – I feel again the emptiness of a life she would have liked, if she could, to fill with that strong happiness in which she moved so effortlessly herself.

David Thomson thought, when he first introduced me to the

Features Department, that Gilliam would soon give me a producer's job. But this did not happen. We did not hit it off. I could not feel at ease with this apparently masterful, efficient, 'dynamic' man in authority. So I went on doing odd jobs as a freelance, a precarious life.

I met such great ones as Louis MacNeice, Dylan Thomas, Elisabeth Lutyens, the celebrated, somewhat shrewish composeress, the more acceptable composer Humphrey Searle and many others, and drank with them in The George and its convenient annex the 'ML' Club across the road, where we could carry on drinking through the afternoon until The George opened again. I occasionally stayed in what might be called the Features Department's 'safe house' on the river at Wapping, where 'Bertie' Rodgers acted as a sort of resident warden and all approved people could stay – a great boon to secret lovers. This alliterative poet, so out of fashion now and perhaps sunk for ever, provided much quiet amusement. He had been a dissenting minister in Ulster until MacNeice, discovering his poems, brought him into the convenient haven of the BBC.

Rodgers, though 'irresistible to women', still had something of a minister's gravity of speech. He specialised in gnomic utterances ('You know what's what and you know where's where and you know when's when; but you never know why's why'). He also had the gift, sometimes found among Irishmen, of being in two places at once. Inadvertently opening his bedroom door one morning I found him in bed with a woman and quickly withdrew to the bar of the neighbouring pub, where he sat quietly drinking a glass of Guinness and asked, vainly, if I could lend him 7s. 6d. Not long after this, he 'ran off' with the beautiful wife of the powerful Gilliam, who was thus shown to be less powerful than I had thought. 'Bertie' had to resign, of course, but continued, under MacNeice's aegis, to work as a freelance. But Gilliam had pronounced a curse upon him: 'You shall be happy, but write no more poetry.' I hope he was happy. It is true he wrote no more poetry of any merit after 'Europa and the Bull' – you are to imagine that pronounced in an Ulster accent – and some years after died of cancer in America. But Gilliam had died of cancer before him.

As for death, my brother had died in the great polio epidemic of 1947 – astoundingly, for his was the only case for fifty miles around his farm at Ambleside – but not before my mother, aggrieved and unable to get on with her daughter-in-law, moved to a cottage in the Yorkshire Dales, not far from the domains of my sister's formidable, Alsatian-loving Scottish protectress, who frightened my mother out of her wits. Her son, who had trained as an RAF pilot in Rhodesia, married my sister, and after he had taken a late degree in geology, they went back to that white man's paradise to live, she to breed pekinese dogs, he to become, in due course, Professor of Geology at the University of Rhodesia.

My former wife had now come to England and, I am glad to say, found a second husband, a good swashbuckling New Zealander, which took away whatever guilt I may have been capable of feeling. My son stayed with his grandmother in Yorkshire – a strange sort of upbringing indeed. But although he must have heard much talk of past glories, of the grandeur of 'Duchy Grange' – a few Chelsea china figures, a glass-topped table, a few plates, said to be of inestimable value, still remained – of his grandfather's foolish behaviour which had reduced them to this humble plight, and, above all, of the Missing Will of the Whartons, he survived to go to Skipton Grammar School and Christ's College, Cambridge, and to keep an insatiable curiosity about his real, or in default of that, imaginary antecedents.

The break with Anne came when we moved from Hampstead (my friends, on leave from Nigeria, needed their flat). We rented, as a temporary base, a house in Holland Park belonging to a young film-producer and his wife. I fell for the wife, Laura, instantly and heavily. She was small, with a well-bred prettiness, fond of drinking and nonsensical jokes. Both, like almost all the people in the film unit he worked for, were 'fun communists', she entirely for the fun, he out of some curious conviction, perhaps connected with his having a very rich father. While they were away, Anne, not without complaints on my part, for I had got used to her and wished to eat my cake and have it, moved out. When they got back it seemed the most natural thing in the world to these agreeable, easygoing people that I should stay on in a basement-room they had made comfortable for some vaguely-projected lodger who never appeared.

We became great friends. The film-producer had, of course, noted that I had fallen for his wife, but, as he told her and she duly reported to me, he thought me much too shy and reserved to tell her so. This was not so at all. Now began the only experience I have ever had of true, romantic and what seemed perfectly requited love. I also found, as others have done, that I had less purely physical pleasure with a woman I loved and cared for than with other women, both before and since, whom I have not greatly cared about.

But this did not matter or cause me to repine. What mattered was the good, warm feeling of being together with this delightful woman. She was wayward, and this, by ensuring that I could never be certain of what she would do next, made her twice as fascinating. There was the attraction, too, of keeping the affair a secret. To arrange occasions for making love involved ingenious stratagems such as taking a room at the Great Eastern Hotel under a false name, or meeting at Rye on some pretext and staying in some freezing hotel, where, in those days of austerity, the food was appalling and the mattress damp and hard. At one time I rented a small room in another part of Holland Park and there we would meet for an hour or two.

There were misunderstandings, quarrels, delicious reconciliations, narrow escapes from detection. We communicated by leaving notes in an unused tooth-mug in the bathroom ('per mugpost') and this is how our affair was eventually discovered by the husband, as

177

it was bound to be. There was a mild scene only – it was certainly not the first time she had been unfaithful; but, of course, I had to leave. I took another room not far away (in those days there were still plenty of bed-sitters to be had), and so my state of happy misery went on.

All this time I had to find money to live on. I wrote odd scripts for the BBC. One evening in 1949 I was sitting in The Stag drinking a pint of beer when a Scotsman whose name I have forgotten came in and asked if there was anyone there who would care to write a script or scenario for the electrical power generation section of the industrial section of the Festival of Britain. This, then in the first stages of planning, was due in 1951, centenary year of the Great Exhibition. 'Putting the "Great" back into Great Britain' and many other inane slogans were floating about. The fee for the script was £150. I accepted the Scotsman's offer at once.

I knew absolutely nothing about electrical power generation but was good at research, as I had proved as a cadet at Catterick. I was given a ticket for the Library of the Institute of Electrical Engineers. There I asked the librarian to recommend a few elementary works. He produced a few and I took them away to a remote desk. All were completely unintelligible. But I had noticed a shelf containing such books as *Every Boy's Book of Electricity* and furtively taking these, I began my research. Every time the librarian came near I had to cover up the boys' books with the books he had given me. It was like being back at school again. But I soon found I was getting interested in the history of electrical generation. It started with amber, the loadstone and the terrible iron mountain in the *Arabian Nights*, which sank ships by drawing out all their rivets if they came near it, and progressed by easy stages to Faraday, that saintly man who, if he could have foreseen the evils his electro-magnetic discoveries would make possible, from pornographic films to nuclear weapons, would surely have destroyed his laboratory and hanged himself. Soon I had mastered the basic principles. I worked on the project, on and off, for more than a year. Not being able to afford the rail fare to Glasgow, where this section of the Exhibition was located, I never saw the humming, clanking, booming end-product of my work. But even now I retain enough of what I learned then to be able to pose, if only for a few minutes, as an electrical engineer.

Another job I was working on at this time was editing the Football Association Yearbook, published by a small firm which had been infiltrated, for reasons I could not discover, by Marxists. One of them, a big, jolly, very agreeable man, was a friend of my Holland Park patrons, who (before the exposure) recommended me for the job. I did not know much more about football than about electrical power generation. But there was less to know. So for the earlier part of 1949 I was busy, when not at work on broadcasting scripts or electrical affairs, on pasting up 'dummies' of the Yearbook, checking lists of results and even writing contributions of my own. My short article, 'Some Aspects of the Offside Rule' (with diagrams), was thought at the time to be the most lucid and masterly exposition of the subject which had ever appeared. I also wrote a number of histories of football clubs, such as Accrington Stanley and Luton Town ('the Hatters').

This meant 'research'. For this I used to go, every now and then, to the Football Association headquarters in Lancaster Gate, in Bayswater. The President of the Association was then Sir Stanley Rous. I never actually met him but those below him in this curious hierarchy of football officials were greatly in awe of him. I heard many stories of his overbearing character. At one time he had declared that the badge of the England international football team must be eleven lions. The College of Heralds ruled that this was a heraldic impossibility. This threw Sir Stanley into such a titanic rage that he flung a heavy presentation inkwell at a subordinate and shut himself up in his personal music-room to play thunderous chords on the organ he had had installed there until his nerves were calm enough for him to enter the human world again. Did I invent all this? Yes. But some of the minor officials almost believed it. I was taking notes like mad at that time.

My contact for research purposes was the Archivist, a Yorkshire-man who lived in a room full of books and memorabilia which covered the whole history of football from its beginnings. He also collected all stamps connected with football (as the game spread to foreign parts more and more of these were appearing). His albums, which he showed me with great pride in the intervals of putting me right on some historical detail or other – who, for instance, played goal for Bradford City in 1913? – must have been quite valuable. I thought of knocking him out, seizing them and making a dash for it. But the thought of the titanic Sir Stanley deterred me. One day when I was with the Archivist, there was a prolonged pause in the conversation (a common experience with me). I was going to say something about Wolverhampton Wanderers when I noticed that the Archivist's face had gone blank and stony. Suddenly, in a strange, indescribable tone, he said: 'I hate Sir Stanley.' I thought it best to make no comment, and in a moment he was himself again and reaching for his stamp albums.

There was one item of unchanging ritual in these visits to the Archivist. Each time, before I left, he told me a single dirty story. Some of them were quite ingenious. Had he invented them himself? Was this strange office the place where all these stories, told by commercial travellers (as they were called in those days) all over England, had their origin? I never found out.

So it was, in these humble, disparate and incongruous tasks, that I kept alive. In desperation, I had also started writing short pieces of humorous fantasy for *Punch* again (there was a whole series about a surrealist boilerworks which I sent in week after week until the Editor – I think it was the one before Malcolm Muggeridge – grew tired of them). The fees, I noted, were somewhat higher than they had been in my days in Westmorland. But living in London was much more expensive. Though unbelievably lazy in retrospect, I must actually have been working quite hard, if to no particular purpose.

Meanwhile I was making new friends and acquaintances in the pubs of the BBC. One of them was René Cutforth, a big man with a special kind of grating voice, one of the most entertaining people I have ever met, and, for all his vagaries, one of the most lovable. He was as fond of fantasy as I was and had invented a monstrous saga of his upbringing as son of a mine owner in legendary Swadlincote, in the Derbyshire-Leicestershire coalfield. But his real life was fantastic enough. He had had an adventurous war, in the Abyssinian campaign and elsewhere, ending up as a prisoner of the Germans. He was perhaps the best of the BBC's war reporters (he wrote a book about his experiences in the Korean War which is by far the best I have read on that subject). But because of his adventurous and irregular life the administrators of the BBC ('the greymen', as we called them) regarded him with suspicion. They did not realise, or if they realised, did not respect, his considerable literary talent. And René himself, when he could have been writing remarkable books, preferred to put his talent into talking, singing and entertaining (he was a prodigious mimic – his Australian and Ulster accents were unsurpassed in my experience). He was, in a way, a tragic figure. It still annoys me to think of all the little people who at that time and since made a reputation as writers with no more than a modicum of his talent. But perhaps – and this is a phrase that often comes to mind – it does not really matter anyhow. He was himself.

Another character of those days who was decidedly himself was Peter Duval Smith, a young man of South African origin, who, according to legend, had been found by Louis MacNeice asleep in a gutter in Athens and brought back to join the BBC. His unique, mischievous laugh was the outward sign of his character. If Bertie Rodgers and David Thomson were irresistible to women, Peter Duval Smith was more than irresistible. It was fascinating to watch the process at work: it never seemed to fail. I made several notes about it.

This man was also completely careless of convention, and there was nothing he liked better than flouting the 'greymen' and generally defying authority. It was possible, by making friends with some girl in the archives department of the BBC – easy enough for such as he – to borrow one of the 'personal files' which everyone connected with the BBC, whether on the staff or not, had to have. These files would be produced at the annual interview which everyone, including heads of departments, had with his immediate superior. Peter got hold of the personal file of Lawrence Gilliam, Head of Features, his own department.

At the next annual meeting Gilliam had with his Immediate Superior, the 'Director of the Spoken Word' or some such functionary perhaps, his file was produced. The Immediate Superior was dumbfounded. The file proved to contain, among the records of programmes produced during the year and so on, some unexpected notes: 'This man is not to be trusted with messenger boys'; 'the unfortunate incident in the public lavatory at Seaford, though due to a misunderstanding on the part of the police officer . . .' and so on. 'What is the meaning of this?' asked the horrified Immediate Superior. Later Gilliam called the whole Department together and told them that unless the culprit owned up, they would all be kept in indefinitely – or words to that effect. Everybody, including the victim, knew that only one person could have done such a thing. Peter had to resign, of course, but, as in the case of Bertie Rodgers, he still went on working for the Department. The BBC was then, in some ways, a mysterious and admirable organisation. Peter continued his adventurous life until, years later, he died mysteriously in Saigon during the Vietnam War.

Amusing though all these merry pranks could be and pleasant as it was to know such people and share their adventures if only by proxy, I could not claim that I was 'getting anywhere', though now approaching my late thirties. What had become of my ambition to be a 'great writer', to be rich and famous? I was reminded of this one day, when, opening a newspaper, I read a review of a first novel by Constantine FitzGibbon, *The Arabian Bird*. 'A new star has risen over the horizon of the English novel,' wrote the reviewer, giving some details not only of the book but of the author's varied life as an intelligence officer in the American Army, interrogating captured German generals by the score, and of his subsequent experiences in America, Bermuda and Capri, where he was said to be writing a life of his paternal kinsman, Norman Douglas. I was not so base as to be angry at my friend's success. All the same it made me uneasy. I had not seen or heard of him for about ten years. Obviously he had not been crawling about on the surface of the earth since he had left the Army, nor picking up a living as best he could, preoccupied with unsatisfactory love affairs. Far from drifting passively, trying feebly to locate some all too missing will, he had been working to some purpose. I wished I could say the same.

One gloomy morning in December 1949 I was feeling particularly despondent. I had been to see the Football Association about the early history of Nottingham Forest and was on the upper deck of a bus in the Strand, about to alight for a morning's research with the electrical engineers. Things were not going well between Laura and myself. There was a distinct diminuendo, a feeling that 'there was no future' in our affair, as indeed there was not. I had nothing to offer her if she wanted to leave her husband for me; I would probably have been alarmed if she had suggested it.

Afflicted by the sort of feeling I associate with going alone to a public library on a Saturday afternoon, I had just turned to get off the bus when a well-known voice hailed me. It was Constantine. 'Nice to see you again,' I said, amazed and bewildered by what seemed a reversal of the laws of nature. 'Quick, drop whatever you're doing and come and have a drink,' he said. We went to the nearest pub, Henekey's in the Strand, and drank quite a lot of

Guinness. 'I thought nothing pleasant was ever going to happen again,' I said, overwhelmed by this apparition from what I had thought a lost world. He told me he had taken a flat in Chelsea with his new wife, Theodora, gave me his telephone number and asked me to go round that evening.

I was not at first smitten by Theodora, who seemed older than I had expected and had an air of immense sophistication which made me feel distinctly small. Asked what I was doing, I could not say I was doing anything much. It seemed they knew Laura from wartime days in London and had a poor opinion of her. Theodora thought she was 'wet'. 'Why don't you get a proper girl friend?' she shouted. There were difficult pauses in the conversation. 'I'm told you're mad, brilliant and witty,' she went on. 'Can't see much sign of it.' Constantine summed it up: 'The war has driven him sane.'

However, in spite of this unfortunate beginning, we soon resumed our old friendship. Constantine was already working on a new book and they were looking for a place in the country, not too far from London, where they could live with their giant poodle, Minka, and entertain their friends. They introduced me to all kinds of people, mostly literary – Terence Kilmartin, Robert Kee, Admiral Fawkes, Oscar Kokoschka, Arthur Koestler, 'Bunny' Esterhazy, Brian Howard, ex-King Umberto (is this right? probably not). They seemed to have a poor opinion of the BBC people and advised me to escape from that milieu as soon as possible. 'You're getting on for forty,' shouted Theodora. 'Time you got a book published.'

The only book I had written was *Sheldrake*, by this time rather *vieux jeu*, but I still hoped to get it published. 'Write another one,' advised Constantine. 'I don't know anything about anything,' I explained. 'What does that matter? Write about badgers.' He was right, of course. Among the people he introduced me to were a pair of publishers, Anthony Gibbs and Charles Fry, who ran a firm called Wingate, for which Constantine, who had another, more important publisher for his own books, did translations, mainly of the memoirs of German generals which were just starting to emerge from the rubble of the war. Gibbs, son of the author of *The Street of Adventure* and other bestsellers, was a dandified man with an eyeglass and a Rolls Royce, and wrote or had written some really terrible novels himself. Fry, a man of homosexual temperament, was languid and unhappy (he later committed suicide). Owing to a misunderstanding he tried to seduce me in his melancholy box of a flat in one of those blocks in Chelsea which had a depressing service restaurant on the ground floor.

These publishers were not inclined to publish *Sheldrake* (it finally got published, in 1958, by Anthony Blond, a rich Jew who joined their firm and then took it over). What they did was to put me in the way of ghost-writing. It did not pay well, but I added it to my list of miscellaneous fringe occupations. I ghosted one book, *Dare to be Free*, by W. D. Thomas, an excellent story, when re-written by myself, of the author's adventures after his escape from a German prison-camp in Crete. It was quite a success. 'Reads in parts like an enthralling fairy story,' said one review. 'Here is that most unusual thing, a man of action who can write.'

Gibbs and Fry also introduced me to Helga Greene, the divorced wife of Hugh Greene, later to be Director-General of the BBC. She was rich (what was described as a 'real', that is, 'banking' Guinness) and then held strong Leftish views. She was rather stern, too, and put me through a cross-examination about my own views before giving me work (yet another subterranean, mole-like activity) in the literary agency she ran from her house near Eaton Square. When I told her my political views, which were as decidedly 'right-wing' as they always had been, she obviously did not believe me. She was one of those people whom I came to think of later as 'Hampstead thinkers'; it was typical of them that they simply did not believe that a person who seemed intelligent and educated could have opinions different from their own. This was convenient for me because she was willing to give me work to do, mainly reading manuscripts. Later on she got me the job of editing the transcript of the Hearing in the Case of J. Robert Oppenheimer, the American nuclear physicist who was suspected of being a 'security risk', on the whole, I think, rightly. This meant reducing about a million words to a book of 80,000 words. I found this task, gruelling though it was, quite fascinating; what I was left with, in the end, was a play. I was pleased with my work on this, and pleased also that the short introduction I wrote for it was described by a reviewer in the *New Statesman* as 'surprisingly right-wing'. It was surprising to him, all right; he was another 'Hampstead thinker'.

For all her brusqueness Helga was kind to me. She even lent me her house to stay in once or twice. It was extremely comfortable. But, fortunately perhaps, she had locked up all the drink and there was nothing to eat either for me or for some girl I took there once except strawberries and a large tin of those cocktail biscuits made in the shape of small footballs with cheese inside. During the night the doorbell had some kind of seizure and went on ringing for hours. My knowledge of electrical power generation proved useless. Fearing that policemen or others might investigate, we fled at dawn.

In the spring of 1951 Constantine and Theodora found the house they were looking for: an old converted farmhouse called Sacombe's Ash, roomy enough and with a pleasant garden. It was in a part of Hertfordshire between Sawbridgeworth and Much Hadham which, considering how close it was to London, was still surprisingly rural, with old-fashioned pubs full of genuine 'characters' and surviving examples of genuine folk art, such as four stuffed squirrels playing cards in a glass case. Constantine and Theodora soon became 'characters' themselves, as they effortlessly took over the local pub, objects of amazement to the rustic customers, who had never before come across people who seemed to belong to the middle or upper class, yet drank their pints of beer and gossiped with the rest.

The pair of them very soon took charge of my life, allotting me a room in their house to live in at weekends for a small rent or none at all; and, since I had to be in London some of the time, they even found me a lodging in a house in Chelsea belonging to the wife of an eccentric would-be author about ten years older than myself. We got on well until my tendency to hopelessness got on his nerves. The part of the house his separated wife allowed him had one unusual feature: kitchen, bathroom and WC were one. It was possible to make toast while sitting on the lavatory.

I spent most of my week-ends with the FitzGibbons. I would sit in my room with a typewriter for an hour or two in the mornings, but had little to show for it, except a large number of disparate Chapters One of my new novel. The house was full of comings and goings. Theodora was a superb cook (she later became a famous cookery writer) and a splendid homemaker and hostess. The FitzGibbons had a great many friends whom they had got to know in their wanderings. Some, like Manes Sperber, one of those central European novelists who had turned away from Communism and wrote novels about the process, were famous in their day; others, like Noel Annan, Patrick O'Donovan, John Raymond, Christopher Ewart-Biggs and Woodrow Wyatt, were to become well-known in different fields.

I have always felt uneasy in the company of famous, successful or powerful people (except in the Army, when I knew, by reference to my shoulder-badges what my own precise status was); later a percipient woman friend said she had noticed how I used to 'climb immediately into my personal dustbin' when such people were about. Theodora soon noticed this too and was inclined to tease me or, in her uninhibited way, call me 'idiot'. I did not like this much. Nor did I greatly like the violent rows the pair of them had together, though these had their amusing side. It is a fact, I think, that when working-class people throw bottles and crockery at each other they quite often score hits; middle- or upper-class people seldom, if ever. Bottles flung by Constantine and Theodora at each other almost always hit the wall behind the target area. However there was the danger of fragmentation, and they usually made sure there was a first-aid box handy. In one of these rows, which were really like tableaux or short dramatic performances (recalling my father's, though on a larger scale), Constantine, after hitting his wife on the head with a heavy German dictionary, sat her on the fire. She came back strongly with a wine-bottle and later they administered first-aid to each other for the cuts and burns they had sustained, laughing heartily and quite good friends again.

There was a good deal of serious drinking, either at the pub, which had a pleasant green space in front of it, arranged with benches and tables, or at the house itself, or, occasionally, at a wonderfully seedy 'country club', a small, decayed house in an overgrown park a few miles off, where the manager, usually very drunk himself, took a tolerant view of drinking and amatory matters. Guests at the FitzGibbons' frequent, enjoyable parties were sometimes boarded out there.

Another agreeable part of life at Sacombe's Ash was croquet. Constantine was extremely good at this and almost always won, even with a weak partner. Though I am very fond of the game, I have never been very good at it; lacking a logical mind (it is a game which calls for intelligent planning ahead and a feeling for geometrical relations), I am decidedly erratic, sometimes abject, sometimes positively brilliant. One great advantage of croquet is that it is the only outdoor game which can be played while drinking and talking.

Both the FitzGibbons were great talkers – an advantage for me because unless I am quite drunk I tend to be tongue-tied or even unable to think of anything to say. Much of what they talked about – foreign places, famous people they had met – meant little or nothing to me. A good deal of what Theodora talked about seemed far-fetched, but was not less entertaining for that. Her father, it seemed, had been an eccentric Irish peer. She had been brought up in one of those great decaying Irish country houses – where it actually was in Ireland I was not and am not sure – with no less than nine gigantic Irish wolfhounds to protect her. These and other details I absorbed without comment, just as I absorbed the continual references to Picasso, Jean-Paul Sartre, Albert Camus and the painters Peter Rose-Pulham (a former lover of Theodora's) and Sir Francis Rose, a man of homosexual tendencies.

After a stay with the FitzGibbons it felt odd to travel north, as I occasionally did, to see how my mother was getting on in her cottage in Yorkshire. When I first went there, 'Aunt' had been sent for to keep her company and, to some extent, to resume her old role of domestic slave. There was no talk about Picasso there. Neither of the two women had ever heard of him, any more than they had heard of Wingate's the publishers, Jean-Paul Sartre, Sir Stanley Rous of the Football Association, Louis MacNeice of the BBC, my friends the fun-communist and his delightful wife, or any of the characters in the different spheres I was living in simultaneously. But my mother was pleased about my job with the BBC ('I'm sure you'll get to be an announcer one day, if you work hard').

'Aunt' was dying of cancer, and very soon had to keep to her room. One of the things in my life, and they are many, I am ashamed of is that I did not go to see her until it was too late – for the day came when an ambulance arrived to take her to Leeds General Hospital, where she died. This was a simple soul; she had no power to harm and so did none; but I do not think she would have done any if she had had the power. She had been kind to me. I never returned that kindness. It is, however, I who will have to pay for that, if any payment is required. Such people as 'Aunt', to whom nothing memorable had ever happened in all her sixty odd years of life, are as great a mystery as Theodora FitzGibbon, to whom amazing things never seemed to stop happening – perhaps a greater.

Life at Sacombe's Ash that summer was an idyllic time in many ways. Things improved for me after a day when Theodora and myself, leaving Constantine to work at his writing, stayed rather a long time in the pub and, returning with a load of vegetables which the locals had provided, fell off our bicycles at the bend in the road. Bicycles, vegetables and ourselves lay spilled in a confused heap and we could not stop laughing for half an hour. After that we got on quite well together. She became even more concerned, in a genuinely worried way, at my lack of a regular girl friend. My affaire with Laura was rapidly fading out. The FitzGibbons, in their kindness, produced several candidates for my love. But none of them appealed to me. 'You are hard to please,' they said. However, their wish for me was soon to be granted, though not quite in the way they might have wished.

Although they were unfailingly kind to me, I felt sometimes that I was outstaying my welcome. Finding that David Thomson, who had a flat in Portland Place, near 'BH' itself, had a couple of rooms to let, I left my base at Sacombe's Ash as well as my base in Chelsea and with my few effects – there were hardly more of them than when I left the Army – moved into a little attic space of two rooms, approached by a rickety old lift and a steep flight of stairs, high up above the roofs of London, in the autumn of 1950.

Work for the BBC, of the same nondescript kind as before, now took up more of my life. I saw more of David and his friends, spent more time drinking in The Stag and The Windsor Castle, a tiny pub in the mews behind Portland Place, and generally distanced myself a little, though by no means altogether, from the grander world of Sacombe's Ash, which scarcely touched the BBC at any point.

I was beginning to feel a curious restlessness and a deepening depression. When I was at Sacombe's Ash, where I still often went at week-ends, I wished I was in London, and vice versa. I went to Yorkshire to see my mother and my son, now thirteen. His own mother, my former wife, also stayed there occasionally (I am not sure how we all fitted in). She was soon to marry her New Zealander and I found we got on better than we had done before, in a perfectly platonic way, of course, but one which may have caused him slight uneasiness. But soon I found the same restlessness, the same wish to be elsewhere, the same depression. I had been intermittently depressed all my life. But this depression was subtly different. I seemed to be sickening for something, as 'Aunt' would have said.

One morning in November 1951 I was drinking in The Stag when a remarkable-looking girl appeared, a protégée of 'Reggie' Smith, a man of many protégés who is well described in the novels of his wife, Olivia Manning. This girl, whose name was Kate Derrington, had hitch-hiked from Birmingham, where her large Roman Catholic family lived, in order to meet people in the BBC and perhaps find writing work to do (she was a poet, I gathered). She was twenty years old, tall, blonde, with a slim, rather boyish figure and a wild, nervous manner. She smoked incessantly and her fingers were strongly stained with nicotine. Her fingernails were very dirty, and her shabby green corduroy clothes and general air of defiance and unconventionality anticipated the mass-hippie movement which was to come. But she was no ignorant hippie. She loved poetry and music and talking about them, and her eager manner was appealing. I felt there was something dangerous about her. That did not make her less attractive to someone who, though inherently cautious, was capable of impulsive acts.

After getting some promises of work from 'Reggie' and returning to David's flat for some more drinks with myself and others, she left as suddenly as she had come, to hitch-hike back to Birmingham and her disapproving parents. I was intrigued, but not 'in love'. But I did not forget her. It was not long before she paid a second visit to London and, without surprise, we found ourselves in my attic and in bed. She said she was in love with me. I did not say I was in love with her. But I found her very attractive and acted accordingly. Making love is a very good antidote to depression. There were other occasions. It was some time towards the end of February (to place it historically, it was about the time King George VI died) that she told me she was pregnant. She seemed, in her wild way, to be pleased. Did she expect me to be pleased? Possibly. But I was not.

A BBC friend of mine lived in a tumbledown farmhouse in the thickly wooded country north of Newbury which is still attractive although it has been bisected by a motorway. His wife, one of the three Irish sisters David Thomson had once been reputedly in love with, was away with their children for a time and he asked me and René Cutforth to spend the weekend with him and do some walking and drinking. In the ordinary way I would have found this enjoyable. But as I travelled in the train to Newbury, where I was to meet the others and then take a bus further on, I felt a deepening depression, deeper than any I had ever felt before. We met, went on to our friend's house, had some supper and a few drinks, then went to bed. It was a primitive old house, lit by candles and small oil lamps. It was cold, and the wintry woods pressed round it on every side. How much of this cold, this sense of pressure was within myself?

I blew out my candle and composed myself for sleep, thinking I would feel better in the morning. But in that instant my mind seemed to give way, to turn upside down and then become a void. Into that void, or out of that void, I could not say which, flowed an extreme terror which seemed to fill every part of my being. I sprang up, lit the candle with a trembling hand and flung open the small window, shaking and gasping. Did I hope to let the demon out? Had I gone mad? Was this what madness was like? Why had it seized on me, now, here? Was the house haunted? These thoughts passed rapidly through what I was trying desperately to hold on to: my conscious mind. I said the Lord's Prayer. I tried to remember some of the poems I liked best and force myself to repeat them. At all costs I had to regain control. At last – I do not know how long this struggle lasted – perhaps no more than a few minutes – I felt a little calmer, though my hands, feet and genitals were cold as ice – a sign, I remembered, of demonic possession. To be able to put a name to what I felt was some sort of help. I got back into bed, sat upright for a long time, staring at the flower-pattern on the peeling wallpaper, before venturing to blow out the candle and entrust myself to the dark. At last I fell asleep.

When I woke, I felt an indescribably leaden sensation, as though all meaning had been drained not only out of myself, but out of all the things around me, the whole world. I went downstairs but could eat no breakfast. If there was anything odd about my manner my companions showed no sign of noticing it. I have always been known for long periods of silence. Someone suggested, after a bit, that we should take a walk through the woods to the pub in the nearest village. I went along with them like a zombie, along those woodland paths which would normally have seemed so beautiful. Now they seemed not to exist, any more than I did. And in that void of no-feeling I felt, from time to time, the onset of invading terror. We drank some beer. I could hardly drink it. We walked back to the house. I could say nothing. I drank a little brandy and felt slightly better. But as night came on I felt worse and worse. I explained that I must leave, must get back to London. Perhaps they were beginning to understand. We walked to another village, waited in a pub for a hired car to take us to Newbury station. In the bar was a television set, probably the first I had ever seen. I stared at it without understanding; the flickering bluish light may have calmed me a little.

The car came; we got into the train; like a dead man I made my way to my attic in Portland Place. David was away. I was glad of that. I did not feel that anyone could help me. Totally exhausted, I crawled into bed and fell asleep.

Next morning, which was a Monday, the leaden feeling persisted. But the inchoate terror had receded. I was capable of thinking. I washed and shaved. I noticed that my shaving-brush had become evil. Evil, a feeling of meaninglessness which yet had a certain attraction, inhered in it. It was as though it had acquired a squint.

These thoughts, because they interested me, were helpful. It seemed good to be interested in anything. I found I was able to get dressed and go to my 'National Health' doctor somewhere off Great Portland Street. I had never consulted him before. He was Jewish, tired-looking and rather seedy. I explained what had happened to me. He did not seem to think it was anything out of the ordinary. 'Yes, run down, bit of an attack of nerves.' He prescribed some tablets – amphetamine, I suppose, the psychotropic cure-all of the early Fifties. I took them 'as directed'.

For several days I had the leaden feeling, though the terror did not return. Gradually I got back to normal, if that is what it can be called. But I have never been free since then of an awareness of that underlying void. It is close to the surface of my life and sometimes, at moments of weakness or tiredness, I feel the onset of that vertigo which, if not quickly brought under control, must break through, invade and possess my being. I have developed certain tricks, such as deep breathing, to repel that onset, not always successfully (I am reminded of the Tibetan saying that by 'method' a man can live quite comfortably even in hell). There are certain associated temptations. One is to invite the horror, to endure it because of the possibility, even the conviction, that what lies on the other side of that evil might be a counterpoising and transcendent good. But I have never had the courage to let go. The other temptation is less easy to resist: it is a certain pride at having sensations, however unpleasant, which are the 'privilege' of a few, the elect, marked off from those who 'smile and call life pleasure'. This pride is, I am certain, very dangerous; it is playing, not with fire, but with evil itself.

At the time of my apparent deliverance from this first experience, I had no such reflections. I was simply grateful to be delivered – by what? Amphetamine? The mercy of God? I told Kate what had happened to me. She told me she had had the same experience herself a year or so before. Was this simply an expression of kindness and love? Probably. It was certainly very good for me. But now the question of Kate and her pregnancy had to be faced again. I would have favoured an abortion – I have changed my attitudes since then – but she, a Catholic, though 'lapsed', would not hear of it. My friends, when I confided in them, gave conflicting advice. Some, in particular the BBC people, advised me not to marry someone they thought wild and dangerous. The FitzGibbons were in favour, especially after they had met Kate and could think of her as a 'child bride', with the 'beauty of the future'. Their friend and mine, Sally Chilver (the Sally Graves I had known at Oxford), who was childless, offered to adopt the baby. Kate, to her credit, would not hear of this.

As time went on, and I remained in a state of indecision, I was attacked by fibrositis, an agonising stiffness of the shoulders. I had read about the German psychologist Groddeck, whom Auden had enthused about in the Thirties; his theory was that physical symp-toms corresponded to mental states or life problems and that popular phrases like 'cold feet' or 'can't swallow that' had literal application. I have proved the truth of this twice in my own life. The moment I decided to marry Kate – it was in a train when I was travelling to the village of Eydon, near Rugby, to write a script about some gamekeeper or other 'character' for 'Jack' Dillon's 'Country Magazine' – my 'pain in the neck', the burden on my shoulders, left me within seconds. Back in my attic in London, where Kate was already living, we agreed to marry. She said: 'I will make your life pure gold.' And what did I reply? Probably something like: 'That certainly sounds extremely nice, I must say.' She was young enough, in love enough, still to find such remarks from me endearing and amusing.

The baby was born in University College Hospital – a girl. We were married just before Christmas in the registry office in Marylebone Town Hall. As we dressed that morning, I mentioned that it would be handy for changing my library books. The

FitzGibbons were witnesses. We were all on the way to being drunk, so much so that the registrar, a true greyman, had to remind us that marriage was a serious matter. The honeymoon, if such it could be called, was spent at the house in the Chilterns of my old friends the film-producer and his wife, who had long since found another lover.

While all this was going on I had, of course, to go on earning some sort of living. Now it was necessary to earn more. I had met, some months before, Denis Mitchell, a features producer in the Manchester branch of the BBC ('the North Region') and had written scripts for him on such subjects as the centenary of Liverpool University and the re-opening of the Free Trade Hall, destroyed by German bombs ten years before. We became friends and he suggested, no doubt bearing my dilemma in mind, that I should join his department in Manchester on a year's contract. I did not much like the idea of living in Manchester, but it would mean a secure job for a year at any rate. I would also see more of my mother and my son, now thirteen and a weekly boarder at Skipton Grammar School. He stayed at weekends in my mother's cottage, absorbing from her rambling talk of past grandeurs and miseries some sense of his own peculiar background and condition. With the appearance of a stepmother only six years older than himself it became more peculiar still.

We arrived in Manchester in the New Year of 1953. I realised at once that Mitchell's attitude had changed. He had the conventional left-wing ideas which were then compulsory not only in the BBC but among all supposedly intelligent people (though there were a few exceptions even in the BBC, notably René Cutforth, who had seen too much of life, including liberation from prison-camp by the Red Army, to swallow all that bigotry and drivel). Mitchell must have been aware already that I did not share those ideas, but we had not talked about politics and so he had not realised how strongly I disagreed with him. He now had a prominent figure of the left, the ballad-singer and playwright Ewan McColl, a bearded man of ruffianly charm, staying with him and writing for his productions. On the evening we arrived, the conversation turned to politics. McColl made some standardised left-wing remark. I could not take it and contradicted him. It was as though I had shouted an obscenity in church.

From that time on, Mitchell's attitude completely changed. He could not, of course, undo my year's contract, since it had been ratified by the Controller of the North Region (CNR) and the Head of Programmes (HP), the diffident, rich, amateur poet and scion of one of the oldest families in England, Brian Cave-Browne-Cave. What he could do was leave me to my own devices. I spent a good deal of time in the Manchester Public Library, doing 'research' on the eight hundredth centenary of the Duchy of Lancaster for a programme which was eventually broadcast with obligatory background music (very agreeable and stirring, always described by the 'composeress' Elisabeth Lutyens, I recalled, as 'cowpat music') from Vaughan Williams's Fifth Symphony.

Meanwhile I was able to observe an interesting phenomenon: the formation, in the North Region Features Department, of a Marxist coterie. The leading spirit was Ewan McColl (a man of talent and ingenuity who, when asked for a bit of a folk-song to liven up some documentary about the Workers, could pop off to the lavatory and be back with a perfectly good one in ten minutes flat). It was noticeable that many of the actors and musicians engaged to take part in Mitchell's productions (one series was the very popular 'Rhythm and Blues', which owed a lot to the American Marxist folk-song expert Alan Lomax and the English A. L. or 'Bert' Lloyd) had the 'right', that is 'left', political views. Some may well have been card-carrying members of the British Communist party.

I put myself beyond redemption one morning in March, when, as was the custom, the BBC people went along at about noon to drink in Yates's magnificent wine-bar, a vast circular chamber like a small Albert Hall, where there were many bars or counters, each with its own set of habitués. I went up to the BBC's counter, where Mitchell and others were drinking and, noticing they seemed stunned and unhappy, remarked: 'What's the matter? What has happened?' Mitchell turned to me slowly and solemnly, and said: 'Haven't you heard the news? Stalin is dead.' I could not help saying: 'Pity he was ever born.' Even in 1953, when the supreme monster's crimes were beginning to be generally known, that might have been an unexpected thing to say even among 'ordinary' people. To these people it was simply blasphemous. They did not speak to me again for a fortnight, and ever afterwards avoided me and also Kate, who, as a wife should, had exactly the same views as myself. If I had gone to Cave-Browne-Cave and told him that a Marxist cell was being formed within his fief, he would have thought I was a madman.

At least things in the North Region were as easygoing in their way as they had been in London. I 'put up' a suggestion that I should write and produce a programme about Lead-Mining in Derbyshire. So for a few months I was able to explore a part of England I had never visited before, the limestone plateaux, hills and gorges of the southern Pennines. This was a district where lead-mining had been carried on from pre-Roman times to the latter part of the nineteenth century, when the seams of lead were exhausted down to a level where it was not economic to mine them because of the expense of pumping machinery. But the spoilheaps of the old mines were full of fluorspar, a mineral which was now becoming valuable. Prospectors were arriving who, by staking a claim under the ancient laws and registering it at the Barmoot Hall in Wirksworth, could acquire the right to work them over.

So that summer I found the means of getting out of Manchester into this delectable part of England, full of 'characters' who became, as far as it was possible, my friends. One of them was John Mort,

a Moravian and former mining engineer who held the office of
Barmaster and presided over half-yearly luncheons in places like
Youlgreave or Ashford-on-the-Water, where clay-pipes were
smoked and there was heavy drinking. There were stories of
eccentric prospectors who, believing that a thousand 'jeeps' in
packing cases had been dumped down a certain disused mine,
surplus of the wartime arms industry, staked a claim there, only to
find they had no means of recovering the treasure. There were
stories of a remote pub where women danced naked on the tables.
There were long, pub-crawling journeys back to Manchester
through those luminous evenings of May when, what with friendship, alcohol and the vestiges of nature-worship, those numinous
feelings, long thought dead, revived. One evening, after we had
been driving all day about the limestone country, questioning various
people about what they remembered of the past, we came to the
house of an old mining engineer, a blank, white-washed building
in a grove of wind-worn trees. He gave us whisky in tea cups. He
played hymn tunes, very badly, on his out-of-tune piano. Every
nook and cranny of his house was filled with mineral specimens.
The level evening light struck through the windows on these
minerals, filling the house with prismatic glory. On the moorland
road back to Manchester there were fireflies in the dusk.

Such was the 'work' I did for the BBC in Manchester. We lived,
first of all, in a horrible hotel near the University; later, in a superior
boarding-house in Fallowfield kept by a landlady whose husband
had died of over-eating; finally in a house in Withington which a
friend had found for us. Apart from the Marxist cell, we made good
friends in Manchester, or rather my wife did, being better than I
was at making friends. The house belonged to Professor Max
Newman, who held the chair of mathematics at the university, a
sarcastic, rather disappointed man, a fine pianist who would 'un-
wind' at night, after his mathematical labours, by solving chess
problems. We and Jane, now a year old, a beautiful child of grave

impassivity mingled with fun, had half the house in return for looking after Newman's housekeeping in term time, while his wife, who did not care for Manchester, stayed in Cambridge with their children. It was slightly humiliating to go into his library, crammed with several thousand books of which I could not understand a single word. He was fond of marmalade pudding and pedantic jokes, i.e.: somebody might say, 'I suppose nobody knows the times of the trains to London?' He would say, 'It is not true that nobody knows the times. It is true that nobody in this room knows the times . . .' This infuriated my wife. We set traps for him so that he might make these jokes. He realised this and made them no more. I grew rather fond of him. There were unexpected things about him. One day a youngish man on a motorcycle came to see him. He looked distressed. 'Do you know who that was?' asked Newman after he had gone. 'It was Alan Turing.' The name meant nothing to me. Now I know that he was the man who is supposed to have invented the computer, a man of homosexual temperament who killed himself, not long after this visit, by eating an apple soaked in cyanide. Such single sightings or meetings with the great or famous were typical of a marginal life.

At the weekends we went by train and bus to my mother's cottage. Those seem in retrospect good times when all or most (my sister's mother-in-law, the Alsatian dog-breeder, was an exception) were good and kind. We rode our bicycles about the country lanes where wild flowers – Canterbury bells, mallow, marigolds, bird's eye primrose, bog violet – were still plentiful. There were millions of rabbits, too, before the evil myxomatosis wiped them out. Kate, walking by herself on the limestone terraces, once saw a rabbit parliament, with hundreds of thousands of the harmless creatures in conclave, their rabbit-elders in the midst.

My programme on the lead-mines was finished at last and broadcast. Very few, I imagine, listened to it. It was the time when television was beginning to take hold. That June we watched the

Coronation of Queen Elizabeth, with everyone else in the village, on the first television set to appear there. Its owner, a shoemaker from Skipton, provided a gigantic tin of toffee for refreshment. Those were innocent times. Who would have guessed that within twenty years this magic lantern would turn into a monster, dominating the lives of whole communities, making people entirely and admittedly devoid of any sort of talent into celebrities, an instrument of evil and idiocy unparalleled in the history of mankind?

In the last few months of that year I worked on popular medical programmes, which enabled me, later on, to pass as a doctor, usually an oto-rhyno-laryngologist, with some success. In the New Year I was told my contract would not be renewed. I had not distinguished myself in Manchester, it is true. But there were other reasons. When I took my leave of Denis Mitchell he did not rise from his chair or make the least gesture of goodwill. Was I not a self-declared reactionary and enemy of the human race?

A low, passive and torpid period followed. For the first few months of 1954 we stayed with my mother. Her initial goodwill towards my wife and baby faltered. She began to remove lumps of coal I had put on the fire in the freezing kitchen. There were telephone conversations ('Yes, I'm afraid they're still here'). But it was only her Yorkshire way. She meant no unkindness. When the old dog-breeding tyrant had tried to bully her into leaving her cottage and taking a much more disagreeable one on her own shrinking estates in the neighbouring village, she had gone and torn wallpaper off the walls. The blame, through some manoeuvre or other, fell on me. While in the BBC in Manchester I received several open postcards saying: 'KINDLY STOP TEARING THE WALLPAPER OFF MY WALLS OR LEGAL ACTION WILL BE TAKEN.'

I applied for several jobs in the London BBC without success. I was extraordinarily bad at interviews. Was this because they, the interviewers at the curving desk, five of them if you counted the psychiatrist, wondered why I, an apparently intelligent man of forty-one, with a varied and not wholly undistinguished life behind me, was in need of such jobs? Did their own feeling that there was something wrong somewhere interact with mine? At last, towards the end of August, a friend of René Cutforth's got me a job in the Talks Department of the BBC, decidedly a step down from the Features, but enough to provide a living. It was a matter of reading manuscripts for their amateur short story programme 'Morning Story', occasionally helping with 'A Book at Bedtime' and 'putting up' and producing various miscellaneous talks. The work was not unlike that of an air hostess: checking the spelling and pronunciation of writers and readers, timing them with a stop watch and generally putting them at their ease. My colleague, James Langham, was one of the last gentlemen in the BBC, a sweet-natured, sad man and an agreeable drinking companion, one of those for whom the BBC provided a refuge from life, and he died, painlessly enough, I think, very soon after he retired from it some ten years later.

The Talks Department had a very different atmosphere from the Features Department, though even that, with the coming of television and the general creeping vulgarisation of the BBC, was beginning to lose its lustre. There was a good deal more politics in the Talks and they were the politics of the Left. The 'Head of Talks', Mary Somerville, was the epitome of such attitudes; if she had known of my opinions, or even of my existence, she would probably have sent me packing. One of the trials of the Department was an addiction to meetings and conferences. Everyone had to attend two or three of these a week. Those who enjoyed them, particularly the lady producers – a special kind of person instantly recognisable but not easy to describe – would have liked to attend even more. They loved minutes and agenda and arguments about inter-departmental rivalries and lines of demarcation. They loved writing little notes during these meetings, folding them up and pushing them to each other across the polished table with its note-pads and carafes of water.

I found these meetings, at which I never spoke unless spoken to, excruciatingly boring. So did John Davenport, who at this time had a brief contract with the Department. A man of note in his day and of considerable influence as a teacher, perhaps the greatest non-writing writer of the twentieth century (he had a literary reputation although he never published a book, and could truly be said to 'know everybody'), he had fallen on evil days. He was a very strong, barrel-shaped man with an incongruous, high-pitched voice of extreme refinement. He was a dangerous man to cross, being one of the few literary men, apart from Roy Campbell the poet, who also worked in 'Talks' at one time, who could and actually did knock people down. As far as I could tell, from the great number of stories about this literary pugilist and from my own observation, he never knocked people down unless they deserved it.

He abhorred pomposity and humbug. Once, at a party, when he was being bored by some high-grade legal personage, he picked him up and sat him on the mantelpiece, saying: 'There; you talk like a clock. You shall *be* a clock. Now tick-tock away.' One somnolent, sultry summer afternoon, when John and myself, after a certain amount of drinking, were at one of the interminable 'Talks' meetings and little scraps of paper were circulating in dozens, he suddenly fell asleep and rolled off his chair on to the floor. There he remained, snoring horribly, until the end of the meeting. Nobody took any notice. For the 'Talks' producers this tasteless incident simply had not happened.

Kate and I were hard put to find somewhere to live, moving from one friend's house to another with our meagre belongings until at last, as so often, the FitzGibbons came to our rescue. An elderly Irishman, Michael O'Connell, had built a roomy wooden house for himself in the woods not far from Sacombe's Ash, near Perry Green, the village of Henry Moore. O'Connell was an old Leftie and friend of old-time Communists. He had invented a special method of weaving and dyeing rugs and tapestries in the big ramshackle shed he had built next to his house. Irresistible to women, he found it easy to get girls in the neighbourhood to work as his assistants on the simpler parts of his processes; it was even rumoured that Swedish and German au pair girls, attached to the prosperous inhabitants of Much Hadham and its environs, had been lured to work for him.

He was just off to South Africa (not quite yet the unique land of white fiends it was to become soon afterwards for left-wing thinkers), so what more reasonable than that I, with my wife and baby, should take over his house in the woods? It was an agreeable place, with a big, gnarled sitting-room and two enormous fireplaces where logs were always smouldering or roaring. It was like Hunding's Hut in *The Valkyries* and it would not have been surprising if there had been an ash-tree with a sword embedded in it, in the middle of the room. It would not have been surprising, either, if some Siegmund had appeared, one night of storm, to carry off my wife. But I was no Hunding, she no Sieglinde, and when Siegmund appeared at last it was to be in another, quite different place.

As well as building his own house, O'Connell had wired it for electricity in a most frightening way. Wires led through holes in the walls to all parts of the house, which had an alarmingly unstable upstairs portion, a narrow gallery with a spare bed. There were several naked terminals which you had to beware of. There was only one master-switch so that you had to have the whole place lit up or have no light at all. In order to read in bed, you had to screw a bulb into a socket above it, removing it when you wanted to go to sleep. It was remarkable how soon you got used to sleeping with live terminals dangling over your head.

It was a pleasant place enough and the country round about was still pretty and unspoiled. It was a two-mile walk through woods and fields to Sacombe's Ash and there – or in the pub the

FitzGibbons had taken over so completely that the landlord was now reading Nietzsche – we spent many convivial hours. Friends came and went. One of them was a saturnine-looking man who was said to be completing a novel. He lived in a house in a wood the other side of Hertford and was a great gardener, fitting little green hoods over his splendid roses against the frost at night and murmuring to them encouragingly. This was Nigel Dennis, whose book *Cards of Identity* was published in 1955, after we had left the neighbourhood, and made him instantly famous. One reviewer, alluding to his exceptionally sharp observation of human fraudulence, said he 'would not like to find himself sitting opposite Mr Dennis on a bus.' But although he was an astringent, even cruel writer, Dennis himself was the kindest of men and looked upon us two and our child with the greatest benevolence.

Another man we met, though less often, was one who had been famous for many years: the sculptor Henry Moore. Unlike Dennis, Moore was a man of great simplicity of character, though there was Yorkshire stone beneath his surface benevolence to all. He had a Russian wife, Irina, a capable and formidable person who must have been a great help to him in managing his life, leaving him free to devote himself wholeheartedly to his work. Once, at a party, he said to me with comical ruefulness, in the Yorkshire accent he had retained, little modified: 'They say I'm a great artist. All these great artists, like Picasso and that, seem to have dozens of mistresses. Why don't I have a mistress?'

Week-ends were spent with the FitzGibbons and their innumerable guests, in talking and drinking to the accompaniment of their few gramophone records. Their musical taste was not advanced. But to this day I can never hear 'Mac the Knife' or other songs from *The Threepenny Opera*, or the songs of Burl Ives, such as 'The Blue-tailed Fly', or that most wonderful of all Irish songs of defeat, 'The Battle of Aughrim', without seeing in my mind's eye that sitting-room and those long-departed friends.

Most days during the week I went to London to carry out my simple duties at the BBC. At first I used to get up early, walk the two miles or so to the station at Much Hadham and catch the train from there, returning in the same way in the evenings. Later we met, through Henry Moore, two commercial artists, the Askews, a childless couple of Yorkshire origin who lived in a rambling old converted farmhouse with Muscovy ducks on a pond and a house-keeper called Cissie. They had a studio in St John's Wood where they executed paintings for various advertisers. Askew himself was particularly proud of his oil-painting of sausages frying in a pan. But his wife was the more gifted of the two, or at any rate more in demand with clients. She it was who painted those scenes of smart people at race-meetings whose purpose was to show off clothes; he was only allowed to touch up the blue sky and fleecy clouds. This led to a certain amount of tension between them, as on one rainy evening when we had supper at their house. Askew said: 'I'll drive you home in my car.' 'How do you mean, *your* car?' said his wife. An awkward silence fell. They used to drink fairly heavily, but were not so good at it as the FitzGibbons, or, to tell the truth, myself. One evening when we were at supper with them after a number of powerful drinks Mrs Askew fell asleep with her head in a dish of mashed potatoes, blowing a fluted channel in them with her snores. Askew looked at her with love, for they were very fond of each other, and said in an affectionate tone: 'Ee, Ah never married that!'

To the FitzGibbons they were a great source of merriment. In this we joined, ungratefully, for they were very kind to us. After a bit we came to an arrangement by which they met me at the end of our lane most mornings and gave me a lift as far as St John's Wood. During these journeys they ate a great many boiled sweets, Mrs Askew continually pressing a large jar of them on me. They were somewhat in awe of my 'education' and general knowledge and the time came when Askew made a regular habit of retailing his dreams of the previous night and asking me to interpret them. 'I dreamed of an old man with a beard and I was eating this beard with a knife and fork when suddenly a big snake . . .' I did my best to interpret them in a tactful way.

There was another way the Askews helped me, though unwittingly. They would sometimes let me stay at their big house in St John's Wood, full of Louis Quinze furniture and purple Venetian glass, when I was late in London and they themselves went back to the country. There were times when I did not stay there alone. Ours was a free-and-easy marriage. I was not the only unfaithful party. We lived in a style which later on became known as 'permissive'. This way of living, innocent enough by comparison with what was to come later, was acceptable when it was confined to a few people and taken for granted among them. It was only when it became democratised and was claimed as a 'human right' by all or nearly all that it became a danger to civilisation.

The time came when O'Connell returned from South Africa and we were homeless again. I did not want to live in London and we had various temporary homes, none for long. In the end we had to give up the pleasant life we had been leading (more pleasant for me, perhaps, than for Kate). We found a furnished 'maisonnette' on two floors in Downshire Hill in Hampstead, one of the prettiest streets in London, and moved there in the early summer of 1955. The house belonged to the painter Fred Uhlman and his wife, who themselves lived in the house they owned next door. We found Hampstead a great change. The Uhlmans did not drink (as far as we were concerned people were divided into those who did and those who didn't). Our first experience with them was an evening party with coffee and little Jewish cakes, at which Fred, who had just got back from New York, read out aloud and at great length an article about his paintings in an American paper. Later there were madrigals. Mrs Blanco-White, an elderly lady, formerly one of H. G. Wells's innumerable mistresses, lectured me on Fabianism, assuming, of course, that I was in favour of it.

Mrs Uhlman was a Croft of Croft Castle in Herefordshire, and
therefore a member of one of the oldest families in England. It was
interesting to observe how her marriage to the Jewish refugee from
Germany had affected her. She was intensely shy and would often
cross the road when she saw me coming, humming, quite loudly,
vaguely Brucknerian themes. In her, pride of ancestry warred with
libertarian and internationalist views. I suspect that if it had come
to a real showdown, pride of ancestry would have won.

Our daughter Jane was now in her third year, a child of angelic
beauty, capable (since she could not, of course, be faultless) of
severe tantrums. Later on, when we took her to France for a holiday
(our horizons began to widen) peasants by the roadside would
exclaim 'Surely this is no mortal child!' or words to that effect.
Meanwhile we introduced her to the sea ('I like him very much,'
she said) and to the moon and stars and enjoyed that vicarious
pleasure which small children can give by reviving our own sense
of wonder at the universe. Perhaps I should say that they could give
it; one of the most fearful of all the evils television has brought
must be the destruction of the child's sense of wonder. What are
called the 'best' programmes – such as those on natural history and
distant lands – are for that reason the worst. I am glad my own
children spent their earliest years without being exposed to this
agent of destruction.

Although we were still visiting the FitzGibbons occasionally and
staying with my mother in Yorkshire quite often – not over fond of
girl children, she was not unfavourable to ours – we made some
new friends in London – John Phillimore, who was to become a
talented painter, and his circle, Nicholas Mosley, West de Wend
Fenton, an eccentric Yorkshire landowner, and others. We gave
noisy parties in Downshire Hill when charades and tableaux were
enacted – one, the Battle of the Somme, brought Fred Uhlman out
of his house and dancing with rage on the pavement in the early
hours. He was beginning to realise that we were not really his sort

of people. But we had rented the Downshire Hill house for three years and were safe there for the time being.

It was an idle sort of life. My duties at the BBC were not onerous, and always I had the nagging feeling that I was using only a small part of my abilities. I was supposed to be a writer. Why didn't I write? Constantine once said I reminded him of a dynamo which was working away without producing any power. 'Never mind; I will write your books for you,' he said. That was kind; but I would have preferred to write my own. Meanwhile I was amazed at his industry, the way he turned out books, translations, even a play, while at the same time leading his busy social life.

I was not entirely idle. I wrote several 'documentary' features on subjects of my own choice for the Third Programme, then at the height of its power and prestige. One of these was a semi-fictional account of my life in Westmorland just before the outbreak of war. Another was about Colonel Sibthorp, MP for Lincoln for some forty years until his death in 1855 – a man after my own heart, a landowner of the old school, xenophobe, enemy of any and every sort of change from railways to public libraries, and to his con-temporaries a comic figure who was continually lampooned in *Punch* and laughed at whenever he spoke in the Commons, which was often and at great length.

Always fond of the British Museum Reading Room, I spent long hours there researching on the Colonel and, because research and note-taking are so much more agreeable than writing, reading everything which had ever been written about him. There, in what poor George Gissing called 'the valley of the shadow of books', I sat on autumn afternoons, distracted on one side by some Central European scholar working on the history of the Bulgarian Exarchate and sucking pungent eucalyptus lozenges, on the other by some tantalisingly pretty Annamite girl student. My head nodded over my books as the leaves of the great catalogue in the round central desk rustled and the fluting voice of Angus Wilson, then Keeper of

Printed Books, later a famous novelist, seemed to come from far away, until I had to jerk myself awake and go out to take a few turns up and down the colonnade with a cigarette.

Another script I wrote for the Third Programme was about the 'Young England' Movement of the 1840s, whose ideas of reviving the feudal system and resisting the 'Manchester bagmen' of Victorian industrialism appealed to me strongly. Oastler, the Tory Radical whose statue stood at the top of Darley Street in Bradford, close to Weir's teashop where Alan Davis and I had met to embroider our fantasies and artificial languages; Ferrand, the enlightened mill-owner of Bingley; fiery Parson Bull, denouncer of Mammon; the great Bishop Philpotts of Exeter – these were my heroes; my enemies such admirers of the 'stream of tendency' as the bluestocking monster Harriet Martineau, who mocked the ideas of 'Young England' as a frail craft of sticks and paper launched by political children and driven into backwaters by the currents of that mighty stream.

I was pleased with the final narration of my programme: 'The "stream of tendency" on which Miss Martineau had lectured them was flowing on, ever more broadly, rapidly and irresistibly. But already, not far ahead, the thunder of unimaginable cataracts could be heard. Even if they had failed, at least they had tried to dam or divert that stream.'

Now it was 1956. Excited by a once famous book, *Outrage*, by Ian Nairn, in which he wrote, with copious examples, of the degradation of the face of England by the growth of what he called 'Subtopia', I 'put up' to my superiors in the Talks Department the idea of a series of six programmes on this subject which would deal with various parts of the country in turn. So for several months that summer I travelled to such places as Norwich (I had never been in East Anglia before and to my surprise was captivated by that antithesis of the North), Dartmoor, Lancashire, the North Yorkshire Moors and so on. Nominally the scripts were by Sir Hugh Casson, a witty gnome of immense charm and a most agreeable travelling companion. In fact I did most of the work (why not? he was a very busy man). By the end of our series of tours I thought I had made a friend, but never met Sir Hugh again. And why should he bother? He knew who was important and who was not; and don't we all, with few exceptions, keep league tables of this kind? Certainly Constantine did; and I, as a believer in hierarchy, had no cause to complain if my place was, on the whole, rather a lowly one.

The completed programmes were broadcast without anybody taking any particular notice of them. But they had been the means of expressing the Luddism and opposition to 'progress' which I have had ever since I can remember. I felt, as passionately as Nairn, a sense of outrage at the ugliness which was overwhelming our country then and has since spread so far that there seems no longer any hope of stopping it. All that is left is a long groan of despair; thankfulness to have been born in time to see something of the beauty and seemliness of England as it once was; and a duty to fight on even though defeat seems certain.

Now came the time of Suez; the preposterous conspiracy of England, France and the State of Israel, and the political humiliations that followed. The BBC people, then as always, were 'left-wing' almost to a man, and passionately against their own country. One evening The George was crammed with producers and other BBC people all buzzing away like furious wasps. I was amused to find that out of the whole crowd only three people had a good word to say for England: René Cutforth, who loved a fight; myself; and a Jewish actor, Anthony Jacobs, who was naturally thrilled by the lightning advance of the hosts of Israel to the Suez Canal. 'On, to Cairo!' he shouted, as others once shouted 'À Berlin!' or 'Nach Paris!' But his voice was lost in the left-wing hubbub.

Now came a great tragedy. It began with a sense of glory, as the Hungarians rose against their Communist rulers, hanged their secret policemen from lamp-posts and burned their torture-headquarters, toppled (most glorious of all, in symbol) the giant statue of Stalin so that only the stumps of the monster's top-boots remained. Then came the return of the Russian Communist forces; the treachery by which walrus-moustached Nagy and heroic Maleter fell into the hands of their enemies and died. In cosy Hampstead we listened on the wireless to those last pleas for help from the battlements of Europe: 'This is where we live; and this is where we die.' There was no help coming to those heroic people, as we knew well. We wept.

Things were not going well with our marriage. My wife was hurt by my neglect and lack of love – or, to be more accurate, perhaps, my perverse inability or unwillingness to express it. Wild and excitable, she made demands on life much greater than my own. For a time, I think, she felt something of that terror of the void which, as I know well, lies close beneath the surface of our lives.

She recovered. We went to Derbyshire for a week, revisiting some of those places we had known as a refuge from Manchester. We returned to spend a weekend with the FitzGibbons, whose own life was not running very smoothly. They had made, a year or so before, two new friends, Colin Welch, who worked on the *Daily Telegraph*, and his beautiful wife Sybil. Colin had started, about a year before, a column of miscellaneous comment, humour and satire, signed 'Peter Simple', the work of various hands, to which I had contributed occasional items (the first one I ever wrote was on the centenary of the death of Colonel Sibthorp). Colin was a very talented and amusing man, a brilliant mimic and of such ebullient nature that on the croquet lawn at Sacombe's Ash Theodora called him 'Spring-heeled Jack'. Through him I met various other people who worked in Fleet Street: Peregrine Worsthorne, Henry Fairlie, Paul Johnson. This was a new world again, quite different from the world of broadcasting in which I had spent ten not very inspiring or profitable years.

The 'Peter Simple' column seemed to me to have great possibilities as a voice of true Conservatism in the British Press, which was then, as now, dominated by the 'liberal consensus' and mostly written by people who held to the 'left-wing package deal', a phrase coined, I think, by the American William Buckley. This package deal included internationalism; faith in the United Nations, to me one of the most enormous frauds in human history; total condemnation of the White South Africans and a refusal to recognise that they were caught in a historical trap and were trying to extricate themselves by constructing a social system which, if it were applied with justice (a big if, admittedly), was not in itself immoral; egalitarianism; pacifism; hatred of the past; and a strange kind of inverted patriotism, an instinctive feeling that in any dispute our own country must always be in the wrong.

Many people who held to the package deal were 'Lefties' who openly or secretly supported the Soviet Union and its policies. Even those who did not had a lingering feeling that the Soviet Union, being 'socialist' must somehow be working on the right lines and offered hope for the future, even though its rulers had committed and were committing atrocities and massacres on a greater scale than Hitler's. They were still suffering too, even if they did not realise it, from the effects of that intensive propaganda of the war years about 'our gallant Russian allies' and the 'glorious Red Army' which still lingered even when the Red Army and the evil system it supported had become an unmistakable threat to what remained of our own liberties.

The 'liberal consensus' at its silliest involved a belief in human perfectibility and paradise on earth. It represented, in fact, everything I abhorred. Colin Welch and I were very much in agreement on most things, though he seemed rather less extreme in his 'reactionary' views than I and did not entirely share my hatred of 'progress'. He was less eager than I to unfurl the green banner of General Ludd (for I was a 'Green' long before the 'Greens' were thought of, and long before the 'Environment' was invented).

The moment of my introduction to the Press was, as it happened, the moment when the BBC was about to be transformed. Television had arrived. The brightest and most ambitious people in the BBC were beginning to 'go over' to it. Nothing would be the same again. That cosy camaraderie was fading. Cracks were appearing in the majestic fabric of 'BH'. Its majesty was soon to be challenged by the new, flashy, gimcrack structures at Shepherd's Bush and Lime Grove. Soon there would be few who could even translate the noble Latin inscription in the foyer of 'BH', with its formal flower arrangements in chaste white urns (the work of a special section of pious and devoted women) beneath the bas-relief of Ariel by Eric Gill: 'Hoc Templum Artium . . .' Later there would be few who even knew it was in Latin.

I have mentioned that it was possible, if you made yourself agreeable to the girls who worked in the Archives Department, to get hold of your own Personal File and examine it. It was about this time that I contrived to get hold of mine. Amid details of the work I had done for the 'Corp' – it was only later that it became known to journalists as the 'Beeb' – I came upon this sentence: 'He is not really BBC material.' An alarm bell rang loudly in my mind. Not long after this I was summoned for an interview with an administrator, a 'greyman' if ever there was one, grey-suited, grey-eyed, grey-haired, grey-minded. He hummed and hawed a bit and then began to talk about changes in the Corporation, the impact of television, reorganisation, retrenchment. He could not undertake to say that my contract – I had never reached the status of 'established' staff, who were unsackable except for the gravest offences, and even one producer, who had exposed himself in the lift to several women secretaries, only got a warning – it would not be fair for him, he said, to say that my contract would be renewed indefinitely. Had I thought about my plans for the future? He thought it only right . . .

I had not thought about my plans for the future. It was not my habit to do so. But now I began to think, not about my plans, for I had none, but about the future. I was forty-three years old. I had done nothing much with my life; I had not 'made something of it' though many people had exhorted me to do so. Apart from my years in the Army (now a lost world, a book closed and sealed), it had been a precarious life in terms of money, status or achievement, a life of odd jobs, a life which when I thought about it, seemed somewhat futile (and so, in a way, appealing to the masochistic side of my nature). It had been a life of self-indulgence marred by an incapacity for enjoyment. I had made little use of such talents as I had. I was even beginning to accept that I had not got any talents to speak of. What had happened to those dreams of being a great writer, of becoming rich and famous, or at any rate famous? The more I thought about my future, as the 'greyman' had recommended, the more unpromising it seemed.

I was staying with Kate at the FitzGibbons' when Colin Welch, who had moved to London with his wife and five-year-old son – the same age as our daughter – arrived on a visit. He mentioned that he was thinking of trying to get a regular full-time collaborator for the 'Peter Simple' column. I made no particular response to this. It was good old Theodora, of course, who suddenly shouted: 'Can't you see, you fathead? He's offering you a job.' 'I never thought of that,' I muttered. 'I must think about it.' I thought about it and agreed to take it. It occurred to me that my humorous fantasies might be turned to better account.

Soon afterwards I had the pleasure of telling the 'greyman' that I had decided to leave the BBC and would be taking a job on the *Daily Telegraph*. He obviously thought it would be a great comedown (so did my mother, for whom, as for most people, a BBC producer, even of the most unimportant kind, had a far higher status than a journalist – I would never get to be an announcer now, and what, after all, was a mere reporter?). But he wished me all success in my new career.

So, on New Year's Day, 1957, after a sleepless night of confused celebration, I sat down for the first time at my desk in the *Daily Telegraph* with one of the most appalling hangovers I have ever had in my life, and without a single idea in my head. I would have been incredulous, if not appalled, if I had been told I would still be there twenty-eight years later, still spinning the faded dream with which this book begins.